SOCIO-ECONOMIC TRANSFORMATION OF SCHEDULED CASTES IN UTTAR PRADESH

About the Author

Noor Mohammad, *(b. 1942)*, after obtaining his M.A. degree in Geography from the University of Gorakhpur with a first class first, joined Aligarh Muslim University in 1965 as a Junior Research Fellow. He was awarded the degree of Ph.D. in 1969 and joined Kirori Mal College in the same year. Since 1976 Prof. Mohammad is associated with the Delhi School of Economics as Lecturer, Reader, Professor, Head of the Department and Co-ordinator UGC-SAP and is teaching geography to post-graduate and supervising research studies in the Department of Geography. Eight scholars have been admitted to Ph.D. degrees and about 40 scholars have been awarded M.Phil. degrees under his supervision. Prof. Mohammad is actively engaged in research in the field of agricultural geography, landuse and planning and population geography and has published more than 5 dozen research papers to his credit in many scholarly referred journals. His books on *Agricultural Landuse in India* and *Caste and Primary Occupations : A Geographical Analysis* have been very well received and have won wide acclaim in Indian and Foreign Universities. Prof. Mohammad has edited *Perspectives in Agricultural Geography* (in Five Volumes) and *New Dimensions in Agricultural Geography* (in Eight Volumes) under concepts International series in Geography which has been well taken the world over.

SOCIO-ECONOMIC TRANSFORMATION OF SCHEDULED CASTES IN UTTAR PRADESH

(A Geographical Analysis)

NOOR MOHAMMAD

Professor and ex -Head
Department of Geography
Delhi School of Economics
University of Delhi
Delhi-110007

CONCEPT PUBLISHING COMPANY, NEW DELHI-110059

Cataloging in Publication Data—DK
Courtesy: D.K. Agencies (P) Ltd. <docinfo@dkagencies.com>

Mohammad, Noor, 1942-
Socio-economic transformation of scheduled castes in Uttar Pradesh: a geographical analysis/ Noor Mohammad.
p. cm.
Includes bibliographical references (p.)
Includes index.
ISBN 8180692507

1. Dalits—India—Uttar Pradesh—Social conditions.
2. Dalits—India—Uttar Pradesh—Economic conditions.
3. Social change—India—Uttar Pradesh.
I. Title.

DDC 305.568 095 42 21

ISBN-81-8069-250-7

First Published 2006

Published and Printed by
Ashok Kumar Mittal
Concept Publishing Company
A/15-16, Commercial Block, Mohan Garden,
NEW DELHI-110059 (India)

Phones : 25351460, 25351794
Fax : 091-11-25357103
E-mail : publishing@conceptpub.com

PREFACE

Scheduled Castes constitute about one-sixth of the total population of India with a lot of spatio-temporal variations ranging from almost negligible to as high as 29 per cent of the total population of the states. Prior to independence and even sometimes later, they had been the poorest of the poor, and socially and economically most backward caste of the country. This could be attributed to a variety of reasons such as illiteracy, social evils like gambling, liquor and litigation, superstition, dominance of higher castes, deprivation from socio-economic status due to their treatment as 'Sudras in the society', stratification on Manu system, inferiority complex against other castes and misuse of privileges and rights constitutionally provided to them. But after independence they are going under social and economic changes both in rural and urban areas. Their attitude towards society and social values and norms has undergone a change. They are gradually not only accepting but have also started practicing certain measures of family planning. They are becoming more conscious about the education and job of their children. Their attitude towards religion, child marriage and superstitions is changing. Economic transformation is also not lagging behind. By and large, they are no longer bonded or permanent labourers. They are now gradually becoming marginal farmers and have started working in non-agricultural sectors too.

But there are a lot of spatio-temporal variations in the modes of socio-economic change among them and their standard of living with regard to structural relationship among sub-castes and social contacts with other castes of the region of their habitation. The scheduled castes residing in urban areas or in urban fringe or even in immediate surrounding urban villages are more dynamic in their social change in comparison to their own counterpart living in remote, distant and rural areas. Educationally they are forward and politically aware of their rights and privileges provided in the Constitution for the welfare of their community. They are now willingly adopting the practice and measures of family planning in order to provide better food, shelter, clothes, education and medical facilities to their children. Socially they are adopting modernity and now they believe more in adult marriage, remarriage, love marriage and even in freedom of women but less in litigation, superstition, gambling, drinking and such other social mysticism. But the rural scheduled castes are in slow process of moving out from the grip of old and traditional bound social values like child marriage, widowhood, superstitions etc. Though the social parameters of these scheduled castes are changing and are taking a new shape, yet conservatism is still prevalent in their society. Hence, their social change is slow as compared to that of urban scheduled castes.

The economic transformation is more rapid than the social. The scheduled castes are no more bonded, permanent and landless labourers. They have become more conscious about the economic gain and returns from their various pursuits. Many of them after getting land by government under different schemes of land distribution to landless, have started agricultural practices and hence, have become marginal farmers. A considerable segment of rural scheduled castes community are now working in non-agricultural sectors like building construction, road construction and its maintenance, factories and in private shops in urban centres within and outside the region. The educated rural scheduled castes now prefer non-agricultural activities and the considerable number of such youths is in banking, marketing, education, administration and judicial services. The rigorous implementation of SC/ST reservation policy not only in employment but also in promotional avenues has given additional incentives to them for white collar jobs. Some scheduled castes have started even their own commercial and industrial enterprises under self-employment scheme of the government. A large number of scheduled castes have been benefited with various schemes of the government such as loans and subsidies, animal husbandry etc. which in turn have brought economic prosperity among them.

Therefore, in this study an attempt has been made to describe and explain the spatial variations in distribution of scheduled castes with reference to their major demographic characteristics; to identify the major social parameters such as education, marriage, religion, family planning programmes, superstitions, political awareness and involvement and to assess the degree of change in them; to identify the major economic parameters such as occupation, standard of living–food, cloths, house, recreation, mode of transport etc. and to assess the degree of change in them; to identify the determinants of socio-economic transformation; to assess the inter and intra rural-urban variations in socio-economic transformation; to suggest practical measures for the upliftment of the socio-economic conditions of scheduled castes; and finally; to suggest a viable short and long term perspective planning for effective implementation of suggested strategies for their upliftment.

The study is based on secondary and primary data. The secondary data related to caste, patterns of landuse, climate etc. have been collected from Census Publications, Directorate of Economics and Statistics and Meteorology Department, whereas primary data related to the theme of the project have been collected by the project fellows for 1510 respondents selected from 30 villages and 10 urban centres. The data collected have been processed and analysed using statistical techniques and have been represented in tabular, map and diagramatic forms.

The book is organized in 7 chapters including introduction and conclusion. It opens up with an introductory chapter including conceptual framework, aim and objectives, hypotheses and review of literatures. Chapter 2 deals with research design, data base and methodology. The geographical personality of the study area is given in Chapter 3 which gives a balanced account of physical, techno-economic and socio-institutional profile of the study area highlighting only those parameters which have relevance with the research theme of the project. The socio-economic structure of the respondents including his personal, household, farming and socio-cultural characteristic is presented in Chapter 4 which is duly supported with empirical data, maps and diagrams.

Chapters 5 and 6 are the core chapters of the book. The former describes, evaluates and explains the social transformation based on the meaningful indicators such as education, marriage, family planning, religiosity, political awareness and involvement, and social mobility, while Chapter 6 deals with economic transformation selecting income, standard of living, housing conditions and exposure to mass media as explanatory variables. Both the chapters reveal considerable changes in all the selected indicators. The last chapter summarising the research work, presents logical conclusions, and gives suggestion and remedial measures for further improvement in the socio-economic conditions of the scheduled caste in particular and rural masses in general for the country as a whole with particular reference to Uttar Pradesh.

Noor Mohammad

Delhi
20th August, 2003

NOOR MOHAMMAD

ACKNOWLEDGEMENTS

At the very outset I would like to thank University Grants Commission (UGC) for providing adequate financial support to carryout this research project. I also express my sincere thanks to all the faculty members of the Department who have given their valuable comments and suggestions throughout the course of this study.

Mr. Sanjay Kumar Agrawal, and Mrs. Rajani Kumari–Junior Research Fellows working in this project have done the entire fieldwork and collection of primary and secondary data. I am thankful to both of them for their painstaking work in the study villages where they stayed for considerable period of time and have collected very valuable primary data. I am also grateful to all respondents of the selected villages and towns, village heads, and the officials of District, Tehsil and Block headquarters. Needless to mention that without their help and co-operation field investigation would have been very difficult. It is the lack of space rather than my sense of gratitude which bars me from naming them individually. I am also thankful to Mr. Praveen Misra and Mr. Sudesh Kumar for drawing the maps and diagrams.

Last but not the least I must thank my wife Mrs. S. Nisa; and my children – Nuzhat, Naved, Zareena and Javed who have provided a very peaceful working atmosphere for the completion of this research project. My grand-daughter Eram Naved deserves appreciation and affection who has always been a source of joy and happiness.

Noor Mohammad

NOOR MOHAMMAD

CONTENTS

LIST OF TABLES

LIST OF FIGURES

1

INTRODUCTION

Conceptual Framework

Scheduled castes commonly known as 'Untouchables', 'Chamars', 'Harijans', 'Down Trodden', 'Dalits', '*Bhangis*', *'Sudras'* etc. constitute about one-sixth of the total population of India with a lot of spatio-temporal variations ranging from almost negligible to as high as 29 per cent of the total population of the states. Prior to independence and even later, they had been the poorest of the poor, and socially and economically most backward caste of the country. In spite of many socio-economic securities provided to them in the constitution and by the government, they are still comparatively less educated, backward and in the dilemma of privilege and exploitation. This could be attributed to a variety of reasons such as illiteracy, social evils like gambling, liquor and litigation, superstition, dominance of higher castes, deprivation from socio-economic status due to their treatment as 'Sudras in the society' stratification on Manu system, inferiority complex against other castes and misuse of privileges and rights constitutionally provided to them. But after independence they are going under social and economic changes both in rural and urban areas. Various constitutional amendments gave rights to scheduled castes. They are also given reserved quotas on various organizations in order to abolish untouchability and other taboos. All these have led to changes in their attitude towards society and social values and norms. They are gradually not only accepting but have also started practicing certain measures of family planning. They are becoming more conscious about the education and job of their children. Their attitude towards religion, child marriage, superstitions, etc. are changing. Economic transformation is also not lagging behind. By and large, they are no longer bonded or permanent labourers. They are now gradually becoming marginal farmers and have started working in non-agricultural sectors too.

But there are a lot of spatio-temporal variations in the modes of socio-economic change among them and their standard of living with regard to structural relationship among sub-castes and social contacts with other castes of the region of their habitation. The scheduled castes residing in urban areas or in urban fringe or even in immediate surrounding urban villages are more dynamic in their social change in comparison to their own counterpart living in remote, distant and rural areas. Educationally they are forward and politically aware of their rights and privileges provided in the constitution for the welfare of their community. They are now willingly adopting the practice and measures of family planning in order to provide better food, clothes, education and medical facilities to their children. Socially they are adopting modernity and now they believe more in adult marriage, remarriage, love marriage and even in freedom of women but less in litigation, superstition, gambling, drinking and such other social mysticism. But the rural scheduled castes are in slow process of moving out from the grip of old and traditional bound social values like child marriage, widowhood, superstitions etc. Though the social parameters of these scheduled castes are changing and are taking a new shape, yet conservatism is still prevalent in their society. Hence, their social change is slow as compared to that of urban scheduled castes. The old and uneducated generations of rural scheduled castes are still fantastic and they consider any change as providential event and as a human choice. The effect of such conservative ideas may be observed in their large size of family as a measure for social security and instrument for generating economic pursuits. But the new and educated generation of rural scheduled castes which is in contact with their own community in urban areas or in the contact of higher castes of the society does not believe in conservative values regarding size, structure and system of the family. The educated scheduled caste women generally treated backward among backwards are revolting against traditional social values. They are now motivated by the glamour, customs and costumes of urban elite. The broad changes affected by religious movements and other process of change such as westernisation, sanskritisation, individual upward mobility of scheduled castes for material advantages, politico-social power and the infiltration of urbanization to remote and rural areas altogether have affected the social life of these rural scheduled castes to a considerable extent.

The economic transformation is more rapid than the social. The scheduled castes are no more bonded, permanent and landless labourer. They have become more conscious about the economic gain and returns from their various pursuits. Many of them after getting land by government under different schemes of land distribution to landless, have started agricultural practices and hence, have became marginal farmers. A considerable segment of rural scheduled castes community are now working in non-agricultural sectors like building construction, road construction and its maintenance, factories and in private shops in urban centres within and outside the region. The educated rural scheduled castes now prefer non-agricultural activities and the considerable number of such youth is in banking, marketing, education, administration and judicial services. The rigorous implementation of SC/ST reservation policy not only in employment but also in promotional avenues has given additional incentives to them for white collar jobs. Some scheduled castes have started even their own commercial and industrial enterprises under self-employment scheme of the government. A large number of scheduled castes have been benefited with various schemes of the government such as loans and subsidies, animal husbandry etc. which in turn have brought economic prosperity among them. Thus there is a need to study the scheduled castes in terms of socio-economic transformation in the society, and the present work is an attempt in this direction.

Aim and Objectives of the Study

The study has many ambitious aims and objectives but the major ones are given below:

(1) To describe and explain the spatial variations in distribution of scheduled castes with reference to their major demographic characteristics;
(2) To identify the major social parameters such as education, marriage, religion, family planning programmes, superstitions, political awareness and involvement, and to assess the degree of change in them;
(3) To identify the major economic parameters such as occupation, standard of living, food, clothes, house, recreation, mode of transport etc. and to assess the degree of change in them;
(4) To identify the determinants of socio-economic transformation;
(5) To assess the inter and intra rural-urban variations in socio-economic transformation;
(6) To suggest practical measures for the upliftment of the socio-economic conditions of scheduled castes; and
(7) To suggest a viable short and long term perspective planning for effective implementation of suggested strategies for their upliftment.

Hypotheses

(1) The level and rate of socio-economic transformation is more among the non-scheduled castes as compared to scheduled caste population.
(2) The level and rate of socio-economic transformation is more among the younger generation than the older ones.
(3) The level of socio-economic transformation is more among the economically well off scheduled castes as compared to poor ones.
(4) The level and rate of socio-economic transformation is more among the urban scheduled castes as against their rural counterpart.

(5) The level and rate of socio-economic transformation is more among the educated scheduled castes as compared to illiterate scheduled castes.

The Geographical Profile of Study Area

The land locked state of Uttar Pradesh, extending over 23° 52′ to 30° 28′N. latitude and 77° 04′ to 84° 38′E longitude covers an area of 294,363 km^2. Structurally it constitutes the part of Indo-Ganges plain which lies between Peninsular India in the south and recently built Himalayan mountain in the north. The plain belongs to the recent period of the geological history and is formed by the sedimentary deposits brought by the rivers of the Himalayas and the Peninsular India. The materials brought by these rivers range from big boulders to fine silt and clay. Geologically it may be classified into two divisions: the older alluvium called Bhangar, and newer alluvium known as Khadar. The former is found at higher elevation and is free from flood, while the latter stretches along the river basins and are occasionally flooded during the wet monsoon months. The entire state is mainly drained by the rivers – Ganga, Yamuna, Gomati, Ghaghara and Rapti which play a significant role in agricultural operations.

On the basis of structure and relief the state is divided into four physical divisions, viz. the Montane Tract, the Sub-Montane Tract, the Ganga Plain, and the Trans-Yamuna Tract. The Montane tract which is now the state of Uttaranchal lies in the extreme northern part of the state including all the hill districts, while the Sub-Montane tract consisting of two narrow belts of Bhabhar and Tarai, stretches along the foothills of Himalayas from the district of Bijnor to Gorakhpur. The Ganga plain, covering substantial part of the state, occupies the central portion and is most fertile tract, while the Trans-Yamuna tract known as Bundelkhand region, lies in the south of river Yamuna. It is a rocky area with infertile soil interspersed with patches of black soil.

The state enjoys sub-humid climate with two monsoon seasons: southwest monsoon season, and northeast monsoon season. The former, extending from mid-June to October is influenced by the humid winds of the oceanic origin and is characterized by the cloudy weather, high relative humidity and heavy rainfall, while the latter is distinguished by dry winds of continental origin, extremes of temperature, clear sky, low humidity and almost no rainfall. The two monsoons closely correspond with kharif and rabi agricultural seasons respectively. The state has variety of soils but more than two-thirds of it is fertile alluvial soil and almost one-third is hill and Bundelkhand soil which are infertile.

It is essentially an agricultural state where more than 80 per cent population depends on agriculture directly or indirectly. Although there are other sources of economy, agriculture is its backbone. The state lacks in power and mineral resources, and hence, in industry as well. Therefore, the economic development and prosperity of the masses mainly depend on sound agricultural base. About two-third of the total area of the state is under cultivation and most of it is irrigated. Kharif and Rabi are two main agricultural seasons. Rice, sugarcane, maize, jowar and bajra are the major crops of the former, while wheat, peas, gram, barley and potatoes are the principal crops of the latter.

Uttar Pradesh is one of the most densely populated states of the country supporting a population of eleven crore with an average density of 377 persons per km^2. It has a very complex population structure specially in case of caste composition. More than hundred castes are found here but the major ones are Brahmin, Rajput, Muslim, Jat, Kurmi, Scheduled Castes, Kori and Kacchi. About 21 per cent of the total population of the state consists of scheduled castes, but they are unevenly distributed. A lot of social and economic changes has taken place among the scheduled castes of this state, but it is not uniform all over it. Hence, it needs research and investigation.

Overview of Literature

The study of caste and its various parameters has been the basic theme of research and investigation of many disciplines such as

Sociology, Anthropology, History, Geography and Economics since long but it is during this century specially after Independence that more studies have been conducted on scheduled castes and their various socio-economic characteristics (Brigg–1920; Ambedkar–1946, 1948; Patwardhan–1973; and Srivastava–1979). These studies which are mainly concentrated on distribution, density and a few socio-economic parameters of scheduled castes, highlight the poverty and backwardness of scheduled castes, (Mukherjee–1989; Pradhan 1986; Sachchidanand–1988; Selvanathan–1989; and Bhatnagar–1990). These studies are entitled as *Untouchables*, *Out-castes, Dalits, Harijans, Down-trodden* etc. which give us general ideas about their poor socio-economic conditions (Lynch–1969; Lal and Tiwari–1977; Vidyarthi and Misra–1977; Joshi–1986; Zelliot– 1992; and Tripathi–1994).

Brigg (1920) in his pioneer work entitled *The Chamars* has highlighted the various socio-economic problems of this caste. In 1946 Ambedkar wrote a commendable book – *Who were the Sudras* in which he has defined the Sudras and highlighted their deplorable condition. In his other book *The Untouchables* he has described the lower status and poor socio-economic condition of the scheduled castes. After a thorough discussion on basic issues and problems he has not only made strong recommendations for the upliftment of scheduled castes but has also suggested several effective measures to achieve these goals. Atlekar (1956) while working on women has identified the position of women particularly the scheduled caste women in India and their participation in different sectors like social, economic, political and cultural. He has made suggestions to improve the position of women. In 1959 Patwardhan has made a significant contribution in his study about 'Chamars', 'Dhor', 'Maharmarg' and 'Holar' – all belonging to scheduled castes community in Maharashtra, in which he has examined various aspects of socio-economic, cultural, religious and political changes in these communities. He has made inter and intra-community comparison also. Alexander (1968) has analysed the social mobility among scheduled castes of Kerala.

In seventies a number of books have been written on various aspects of scheduled castes (Patwardhan–1973; Desai–1976;

Sachchidanand–1977; Vidyarthi and Misra–1977; and Bhardwaj–1979). Sinha (1977) has made a commendable study on scheduled castes wherein he has not only examined the social and economic change in this caste but has also accounted its determinants. Finally, he has given concrete pragmatic suggestions for improving their socio-economic and politico-cultural conditions. Shyamlal (1979) while studying the socio-economic problems and the impact of sanskritisation on the social change, has made a commendable contribution in his study of Bhangis of Jodhpur city. Desai (1976) has made a regional study of scheduled castes dealing with untouchability in rural Gujarat. Lal and Tiwari (1977) have made an intensive study of 'The Harijan Elite' and their role and impact on the society. Mukherjee in his book *The Chamars of Uttar Pradesh* (1980) has described and explained the spatial distribution of scheduled castes and their socio-economic attributes. He has identified the determinants of their backwardness and has done a comparative analysis of the socio-economic condition of scheduled castes with other castes of the society. He has suggested several practical measures for the upliftment of scheduled castes. This study is based on secondary data, which is neither comprehensive nor authentic. Hence, gives very general information about scheduled castes of the state.

The increasing atrocities on scheduled castes and their awakening towards their rights and privileges have created a lot of interest among the scholars of various disciplines in eighties and a large number of books have come up during this decade (Parvatamma and Satyanarayana–1984; Mathew–1986; and Roy and Singh–1987). These studies deal with social status, awakening, socio-economic change and certain schemes of poverty elevation among scheduled castes (Joshi–1982; Yadav–1983; Kumble–1983; Sharma–1985; Singh–1986; Joshi–1986; Pradhan–1986; Sharma–1986; Sachchidanand–1988; Parkash–1989; Selvanathan–1989; and Parvatamma-1989). Similarly, many studies have been done in nineties dealing with almost with similar aspects of scheduled castes (Bhatnagar–1990; Kumar–1991; Zelliot–1992; Danda–1993; Tripathi-1994; Krshisagar–1994; and Massey–1995). Bhatnagar has made a significant contribution by making a comprehensive study of Jatav-chamars of Dehra Dun city. This study has made a comparative analysis of rural and urban scheduled castes and has described their changing socio-economic conditions. The department of Scheduled Caste Development and Training (UP) has also conducted several studies, which have been published in the form of booklets, reports and monographs. These studies also deal with demographic characteristics of scheduled castes with emphasis on their socio-economic conditions and their determinants. These studies based on empirical data have made a large number of recommendations for the upliftment of scheduled castes but these studies are politically motivated. Hence, they do not give the clear picture of scheduled castes. Besides these, a number of social science departments of several universities and colleges have also undertaken studies on certain specific aspects of scheduled castes in their M.Phil. and Ph.D. Dissertations which have not yet been published. Many such studies have been conducted in the Department of Geography of Panjab University, Chandigarh.

From the review of the above mentioned pioneer works conducted on various social, economic, political, cultural and religious aspects of scheduled castes it is obvious that there are still a lot of gaps at regional and national levels. There are very few studies done on the scheduled castes of Uttar Pradesh, and they are entirely based on secondary data, which are neither comprehensive nor authentic. Hence, there is a basic need to study scheduled castes in regional framework from socio-economic transformation point of view. Therefore, the state of Uttar Pradesh has been selected for in depth study in this book.

REFERENCES

Alexander, K.C., 1968 : *Social Mobility in Kerala*, Uppal Publishing House, Delhi.

Ambedkar, B.R., 1946: *Who Were the Sudras?*, Thackers Publications, Bombay.

Ambedkar, B.R., 1948: *The Untouchables*, Amrit Book Co., New Delhi.

Bhardwaj, A.N., 1979: *The Problems of Scheduled Castes and Scheduled Tribes in India*, Light and Life Pub., New Delhi.

Bhatnagar, A.,1990: *A Scheduled Caste in an Urban Setting – The Jatav Chamars of Dehra Dun City.*

Bumble, M.D., 1983 : *Deprived Castes and their Struggle for Equality*, Ashish Publishing House, Delhi.

Danda, A.K., 1993: *Weaker Sections in Indian Villages*, Inter India Pub., New Delhi.

Dutta, N. K.,1931: *Origin and Growth of Caste in India*, Calcutta.

Ghurye, G.S.,1961: *Caste, Class and Occupation*, Popular Book Depot, Bombay.

Joshi, B.R., 1982: *Democracy in Search of Equality: Untouchable Politics and Indian Social Change*, Hindustan Pub. Co., Delhi.

Joshi, B.R., 1986: *Untouchable – Voice of Dalit Liberation Movement*, Select Book Service Syndicate.

Kumar, P., 1991: *Poverty, Election and Rural Harijans*, Discovery Publishing House, New Delhi.

Lal, A.K. and Tiwari, S.N.,1977: *The Harijan Elite*, Thompson Press, Faridabad.

Lynch, O.M., 1969: *The Politics of Untouchables*, National Pub., Delhi.

Massey, J., 1995: *Dalits in India*, Manohar Pub., Delhi.

Mathew, J.,1986 : *Ideology, Protest and Social Mobility:Case Studies of Mhars and Pulayas*, Inter India Pub., New Delhi.

Mohammad, N., 1989 : *Impact of Caste on Primary Occupations: A Geographical Analysis*, Concept Publishing Co., New Delhi.

Mohammad, N., 2000 : Socio-economic Transformation of Scheduled Caste in Eastern Uttar Pradesh: A Geographical Analysis, in Singh D.K., Dube, R.S. and Srivastava, V.K.(eds.) *Geography, Development and Change*, Association of Marketing Geographers of India, Gorakhpur.

Mukherjee, A.B., 1980: *The Chamars of Uttar Pradesh*, Leeladevi Publication, New Delhi.

Parvathamma, C., 1989: *Scheduled Castes at the Cross Road*, Ashish Publishing House, Delhi.

Parvathamma,C. and Satyanarayana,1984: *New Horizons and Scheduled Castes*, Ashish Publishing House, Delhi.

Patwardhan, S., 1973: *Changes Among India's Harijan*, Orient Longman, New Delhi.

Pradhan, A.C., 1989: *The Emergence of the Depressed Classes*, Bookland International, Bhubaneshwar.

Prakash, N.,1989 : *Scheduled Castes : Socio-economic Change*, Chugh Pub., Allahabad.

Roy, R. and Singh, V.B.,1987: *Between Two World: A Study of Harijan Elites*,Discovery Pub. House, Delhi.

Selvanathan, S., 1989 : *Status of Scheduled Castes*, Ashish Publishing House, Delhi.

Sharma, N., 1985: *Untouchables in Rural Gujarat*, Popular Prakashan, Bombay.

Sharma, R.S., 1958: *Sudras in Ancient India*, Delhi.

Sharma, S., 1986: *The Chamar Artisans*, B.R. Pub., New Delhi.

Shirsagar, R.K., 1994: *Dalit Movement in India and its Leaders*, M.D. Publishers,

Delhi.

Shukla,K.S.andVerma,B.M.,1993:*Development of Scheduled Castes and Administration*, Uppal Publishing House, Delhi.

Singh,D.R.,1985: *Rural Leadership Among Scheduled Castes*, Chugh Pub., Allahabad.

Sinha, A., 1982: *Caste System: Myths, Reality,Challenge*, New Delhi.

Sinha, Sachchidanand, 1977 : *The Harijan Elite*, Thompson Press Ltd., Delhi.

Sinha, Sachchidanand, 1988: *Social Change in Village India*, Concept Publishing Co., New Delhi.

Srivastava, S.M., 1979: *Harijan in Indian Society*, The Upper India Pub., Lucknow.

Tripathi, R.B., 1994: *Dalit: A Sub-Human Society*, Ashish Publishing House, Delhi.

Vidyarthi, L.P. and Mishra, M.,1979: *Harijan To-day: Socio-Economic, Political, Religious and Cultural Analysis*, Classical Pub., New Delhi.

Yadav, S.K.,1983: *Harijan Awareness of Educational Schemes*, Academy Press, Gurgaon.

Zellion, E.,1992: *From Untouchables to Dalit: Essays in Ambedkar Movement*, Manohar Pub., New Delhi.

2

RESEARCH DESIGN, DATABASE AND METHODOLOGY

The study is based on both primary and secondary data. The former has been generated through questionnaire and field observation methods, while the latter are tapped from various government and quasi-government sources. The main sources of secondary data are various publications of Census of India, Directorate of Economics and Statistics and so on. Besides these, various reports and documents of various NGOs have been utilized. District and State-level Gazetteers are consulted for historical background.

Based on processing, analysis and mapping of secondary data, regions of concentration and dispersal of scheduled castes have been identified using technique of concentration and dispersal. As such the state has been divided into following four scheduled castes concentration and dispersal regions (Fig.2.1):

(1) Region of High Concentration- > 25%
(2) Region of Moderate Concentration - 21-25%
(3) Region of Low Concentration - 16-20%
(4) Region of Very Low Concentration - <15%

From these four regions altogether 40 villages and 10 urban centres have been selected for in-depth study. However, these villages and urban centres have been selected on the basis of the following criteria :

(1) The village should be, as far as possible, the representative of its own region specially with respect to the concentration

of scheduled castes.

(2) The village should be easily accessible either by road or railways.

(3) Some of the villages should be near the city centre, while some should be away so that urban influence could be examined, if there is any.

(4) They should be uniformly distributed, as far as possible, all over the state.

(5) The village should be inhabited by the other castes also.

(6) The village should be having 100 to 500 households.

(7) In the selection of urban centre almost the same criteria of selection of villages have been kept in mind except the size of the households.

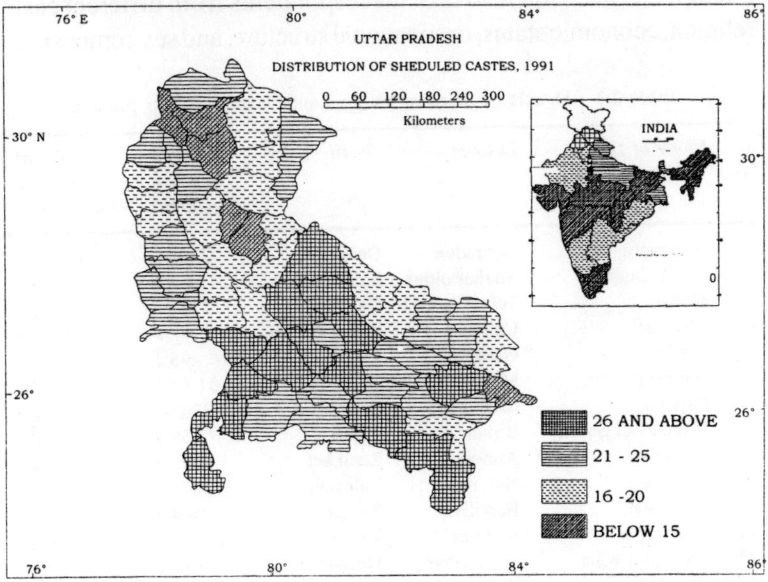

Fig. 2.1

Keeping the above criteria in view, intensive reconnaissance survey of the region was done, contacts were developed with the top level district officials down to the Village Level Worker (VLW). In consultation with these officials, two/three villages were tentatively selected from each region. After a brief reconnaissance survey of these tentative villages, the final village was decided.

Finally, 40 villages and 10 urban centres were selected for conducting field survey (Table 2.1). From each village 5 to10 per cent of the total households were selected on purposive sampling basis. In the selection of the household the utmost care has been taken for the representation of major sections of the scheduled castes. Besides these, their composition, occupational structure, economic status, and sex have also been kept in mind in the selection of the household. In addition to scheduled castes, non-scheduled castes households amounting to 20-30 per cent of the selected respondents have also been selected. These respondents have been selected in order to assess the differences in the socio-economic transformation of scheduled castes and non-scheduled castes population. In the selection of non-scheduled castes respondents attempt has been made to take the respondents from different caste, religion, economic status, occupational structure, and sex composition.

Table 2.1 : Details of Selected Villages and Towns of Uttar Pradesh

S. No.	*Name of the Village/Town*	*District*	*Tehsil*	*Area (In Hectares)*	*No. of Selected Households*
1	Shyampur	Dehradun	Dehradun	222.98	25
2	Sadak Dudhali	Shaharanpur	Shaharanpur	156.21	36
3	Mahar	Tehri Garhwal	Dev Prayag	234.73	20
4	Chaudali	Chamoli	Karan Prayag	118.58	20
5	Suishi	Garhwal	Thailisain	95.1	39
6	Naurara	Muzaffarnagar	Muzaffarnagar	312.02	36
7	Rajapur	Ghaziabad	Ghaziabad	220.97	40
8	Mandawali Saidu	Bijnor	Bijnor	59.9	20
9	Matkhani	Almora	Ranikhet	407.53	40
10	Kamala	Nainital	Haldwani	373.54	31
11	Deoranian	Bareilly	Baheri	344.8	25
12	Mansurpur	Rampur	Rampur	215.3	25
13	Nakatpuri Kala	Moradabad	Moradabad	251.72	40
14	Dharakpur	Bulandshahr	Anupshahr	381.63	40
15	Jaohara	Aligarh	Khair	196.68	40
16	Chaumuha	Mathura	Chhata	2040.5	40
17	Salarpur	Badaun	Badaun	259.41	40
18	Dolapur	Sahjahanpur	Jalalabad	91.46	20
19	Pilibhit Kohana	Pilibhit	Pilibhit	163.9	20
20	Sahdeva	Kheri	Mohammadi	119.79	22
21	Rajapur Puraina	Bahraich	Nanpara	299.07	30

Contd. ...

Table 2.1 *Contd. ...*

S. No.	*Name of the Village/Town*	*District*	*Tehsil*	*Area (In Hectare)*	*No. of Selected Households*
22	Pure Leddi	Gonda	Gonda	55.45	19
23	Khamaria	Bara Banki	Nawabganj	149.74	17
24	Balia Kheda	Lucknow	Mohanlal Ganj	8.9	25
25	Magarwara	Unnao	Unnao	479.57	25
26	Narchha	Jalaun	Orai	268.32	15
27	Rupa Dhamna	Jhansi	Murainipur	661.68	33
28	Kadesara Kalan	Lalitpur	Talbehat	1826.01	35
29	Chando	Hamirpur	Mahoba	592.08	16
30	Palhari	Banda	Banda	620.41	20
31	Beri Gadiba	Fatehpur	Fatehpur	515.99	28
32	Dalmau	Rae Bareli	Dalmau	1449.59	30
33	Mauli	Pratapgarh	Kunda	502.64	40
34	Dorma	Allahabad	Sirathu	113.32	20
35	Mali Mainahan	Sidharthnagar	Domariaganj	314.45	39
36	Maheshpur	Sultanpur	Musafir-Khana	67.58	25
37	Deogaon	Deoria	Hata	86.61	22
38	Gopalpur	Mau	Sagari	225.82	24
39	Khand	Azamgarh	Sagari	131.12	21
40	Newada	Varanasi	Gyanpur	48.56	41
41	Agrawal Mandi	Meerrut	Baghpat	0.92	40
42	Radhakunt Town Area	Mathura	Mathura	0.49	40
43	Agra Nagar Nigam	Agra	Agra	61.8	33
44	Kuraoli Town Area	Mainpuri	Mainpuri	0.47	39
45	Ekdil Town Area	Etawah	Etawah	3	35
46	Orai Town Area	Jalaun	Orai	20.29	40
47	Hansari Gird Town Area	Jhansi	Jhansi	8.95	35
48	Gosaiganj Town Area	Lucknow	Mohan Lal Ganj	3.6	35
49	Basti	Basti	Basti	19.43	29
50	Mugalsarai Town Area	Varanasi	Chandauli	3.89	40

From each household either the senior member of household or the one who takes major decisions regarding day-to-day affairs of family, specially in agricultural matters, was selected. Finally, selected respondents were interviewed in detail according to well-prepared survey schedule. First of all a pilot village-Rajapur lying in the district of Ghaziabad, was selected and the field survey was conducted by Project Director and Junior Research Fellow in order to verify the feasibility and workability of the prepared survey schedules. It took more than a week to complete the survey of this village as several additions and modifications were to be made in survey schedules arising out of experience in this village. After coming back from Rajapur (Ghaziabad), we started checking and rechecking the survey schedules. After being satisfied with entries made therein, we started processing of data, several new problems cropped up. As a result of all these, we have to restructure the survey schedules giving new direction and orientations. A brief summary of the final survey schedules is given below:

Survey Schedules

Schedule No. I : This schedule, besides containing miscellaneous information regarding village, its location, date of interview etc., is for recording personal and household characteristics of respondents.

Schedule No. II : This includes the characteristics of the farming units including land holdings (actual and operational), tenancy system, crop landuse, agricultural problems, agricultural inputs and outputs. It also includes adoption of farming innovations specially farming practices, farm implements, improved varieties of seed, irrigation facilities, chemical fertilizers, insecticides and pesticides.

Schedule No. III : It includes questions related to educational level and the attitude towards the education of children.

Schedule No. IV : It deals with the attitude towards the marriage of the children of the respondent. The questions regarding the inter-caste marriage, age at marriage, dowry system, family planning etc. are included in it.

Schedule No. V : This schedule includes question related to the religiosity in order to assess the attitude towards religion. Questions related to time of worship, place of worship etc. have been included into it.

Schedule No. VI : This schedule includes questions regarding political awareness and involvement. It includes question related to the knowledge about the political situation at local, national and international levels. The question regarding their participation in various political activities and their perception regarding the overall political scenario of the country have also been included into it.

Schedule No. VII : It deals with the mode of transport and the social mobility of the respondents. The questions related to the visits of the respondent to relatives and official, have been included into it.

Schedule No. VIII : This is ment for assessing the housing condition of the respondents. Hence, questions related to number of houses, type of houses, area of the house, building material and household amenities were included in it.

Schedule No. IX : This includes questions regarding exposure to mass media such as radio, television, cinema, newspaper, magazine, agricultural fair and exhibitions.

Schedule No. X : It includes various questions related to means of transport.

Schedule No. XI : This schedule deals with the occupational transformation of the respondents. It contains questions regarding the occupations like dairy farming, piggeries, fishing, labour and poultry farming. Besides this, information regarding services in government/ non-government were also collected through this survey schedule.

Schedule No. XII : It is meant for the general remark by the surveyor based on his discussion, observation and perception.

The interview schedule was organised in such a way that the information may be obtained not necessarily at one time, but over a period of time. In many cases farmers could not spare as much as

30 minutes to one hour at a time, and hence, the farmers were visited on two or more occasions.

The interviews were carried out by Project Fellow having post-graduate and M.Phil. degree in Political Science and working for his Ph.D. dissertation in the first year of the project. The Principal Investigator also carried out field survey either independently or along with Project Fellow. The field survey took more than six months in spite of the fact that Project Fellow and the Principal Investigator were conducting the field survey. The Block Development Officials, specially *gram sevaks* (VLW), revenue officials, local school teachers, were contacted in order to facilitate the interview of farmers in study villages. The Project Fellows stayed in the villages for a week or more so that they could do their best in filling the entries of interview schedules, and also make minute observations regarding various economic and socio-cultural features of the village.

After completing field survey of majority of selected villages, the processing of data was taken up. First of all, a thorough checking of entries of interview schedules was done, and wherever omission, duplication, confusion or any problem was found, and it was not possible to rectify it by any of the above mentioned methods, the village was resurveyed wholly or partially depending upon the gravity of the situation.

However, in order to check the genuineness of field investigators, and also the accuracy of entries made in interview schedules, Principal Investigator has visited several villages on the basis of random sampling. About 10 to 20 per cent of interview schedules were checked and verified on random basis by Principal Investigator himself. Thanks to field investigators that all the information given in interview schedules were found correct with few exceptions which is, perhaps, due to the reporting or interpretation and perception of the problem.

After having been satisfied with entries of the interview schedules by making alteration, modifications and removing discrepancies, the processing of data was done in four ways:

(1) Simple statistical techniques which were possible to apply and workout manually;

(2) Cartographic techniques, wherever spatial pattern of distribution was more important;
(3) Computer technique for working out some of the simple percentages, frequencies etc.; and
(4) GIS packages have been used for preparing maps and diagrams.

In several cases scoring scheme has been used in order to bring the variables at uniform scale. A detailed logical account would be given while dealing with these variables in the succeeding chapters.

REFERENCES

Baily, K.D.,1994: *Methods of Social Research*, Free Press, New York.

Blaikie, M.,2000: *Designing Social Research*, Polity Press, Cambridge.

Brishni, R.W., 1973: *Cross Cultural Research Methods,* John Wiley, New York.

Doi, K., 1957: The Industrial Structure of Japanese Prefecture, Proceedings of I.G.U. Regional Conference, Japan.

Gregory, R.J.,2003: Tribes and Tribal:Origin, Use, and Future of the Concept. *Studies of Tribes and Tribals*,Vol.1, Delhi.

Harvey, D.W.,1969: *Explanations in Geography*, Arnold, London.

Kothari,C.R.,1990: *Research Methodology, Methods and Techniques*, Second Ed. Wiley Eastern, New Delhi.

Kulkarni,K.M.,1977: Micro Level Variations in Economic Development in Rajasthan, *Indian Journal of Regional Science*, No.2,Vol.9.

Kundu, A, 1975: Construction of Composite Indices for Regional Analysis – An Enquiry in the Methods of Analysis: *Geographical Review of India* (1) Vol.37.

Majeed,A.,1992:"Crop-Combinational Analysis: A Review in Methodology" in Mohammad, N.(ed.),*New Dimensions in Agricultural Geography*, Vol.V., Concept Pub. Co., New Delhi.

Newman,W.L.,1997: *Social Research Methods : Qualitative and Quantitative Approach*, Allen and Beacon, Boston.

Pal, M.N.,1975: Regional Disparities in the Levels of Development, *Indian Journal of Regional Science,* Vol.II, No.1.

Pal, M.N.,1962 : *Composite Index of Economic Development: A Method of Regional Analysis of Economic Development with Special Reference to South India*, Regional Survey Unit, Indian Statistical Institute, New Delhi.

Sharma, K.L.,1968: Level of Mobility in Caste Structure - A Hypothetical Refinement, *The Indian Journal of Social Work*, Vol. XXXII, No.4.

Strauss, A.and Gornin,J.,1999: *Basics of Qualitative Research –Grounded Theory Practice and Techniques*, Sage.

3

GEOGRAPHICAL PROFILE OF THE STUDY AREA

Physical Setting

Uttar Pradesh* lies between 23°28′ to 31°28′ N latitude and 77°04′ to 84°38′ E longitude. Punjab and Haryana lie in west and Himachal Pradesh, Tibet and Nepal to its north. The state of Madhya Pradesh lies in south while state of Bihar lies towards its east. The state has an area of 294,363 sq. km., which is 14.42 per cent of the total area of India. Structurally it constitutes a part of the Indo-Ganges Plain which lies between Peninsular India in the south and recently built Himalayan mountains in the north. The region is 400 km. wide in its broadest part and about 2400 km. long in its length, and it covers an area of about 640,000 sq. km. (Krishna, 1960). The plain belongs to the recent period of the geological history and is formed by the sedimentation deposits brought by rivers of the Himalayas in the north and northern Gondwana land of Peninsular India in the south. The sedimentation is believed to have taken place in the Gangetic trough of post-tertiary formation and filled by Pleistocene alluviation. The material brought by these rivers ranges from big boulders to fine silt and clay. The characteristic features of the Gondwana rocks, found on the northern rim of the alluvial tract,

---

* At the time of submission, sanction and collection of data for the project, the state was not divided into two, viz. Uttar Pradesh and Uttranchal. Hence, in this project report it has been taken as one unit.

lead us to believe that its substratum is an extension of the peninsular rocks.

The geological evolution of this plain is a much disputed matter among the geologists. But the common denominator of all the geological and geodetic evidences and theories is that Ganga plain was a sag in the crust formed between the northern drifting Indian continent and comparatively soft sediments accumulated in the Tethyan Basin, when the latter was crumpled and lifted up into a mountain system (Krishna, 1960; and Burrard, 1912). However, the latest theory of plate tectonic is more applicable to the formation of Himalayas and the Ganga plain.

The alluvial deposits of Ganga Plain consists of sand, silt, and clay with occasional gravel beds and lenses of peaty organic matter. It may be classified geologically into two divisions : the older alluvium called *Bhangar*, and the newer alluvium known as *Khadar*. In respect of their age, these deposits correspond with two main divisions of Quaternary era: the Pleistocene and the Recent. Owing to lack of information regarding fossil characteristics of their age, it is difficult to draw any distinct line of demarcation between these two divisions. However, the *Bhangar* lands occupy the higher areas and are not inundated by rivers during the rains, while the *Khadar* lands generally stretch along the river basins and are occasionally flooded during the wet monsoon months.

The *Bhangar* land is rather dark in colour and is generally rich in nodules of impure calcium carbonate which are of all shape and sizes ranging from small grains to lumps of fairly big size. Small patches of saline and alkaline efflorescence are also found in this land. Alkaline formation is explained by the fact that the dominant constituent of the old alluvium is clay and sodium clay, which, after reaching with *Kankar* nodules, is turned into calcium clay and liberates sodium carbonate (Auden and Roy, 1942).

The *Khadar* land occupy lower level which is in conformity with the general principle that as a river becomes older in time, its deposits become progressively younger and if the bed of river is continuously sinking lower, the latter deposits occupy a lower position along its basin than earlier deposits (Wadia, 1976). The *Khadar* is most conspicuous in the eastern half of the state forming a belt of varying width along the bank of Ganga,

Ghaghara, Rapti, Gandak and Gomati rivers. The monotony of the khadar is disturbed by the occurrence of irregular depressions marking the old course of the rivers, some of them resembling tributary valley and others serving as narrow lakes.

Broadly the state can be divided in the following four physical regions on the basis of relief, topography and altitude (Fig.3.1):

(1) The Montane Tract.
(2) The Sub-Montane Tract.
(3) The Ganga Plains.
(4) The Trans-Yamuna Tract.

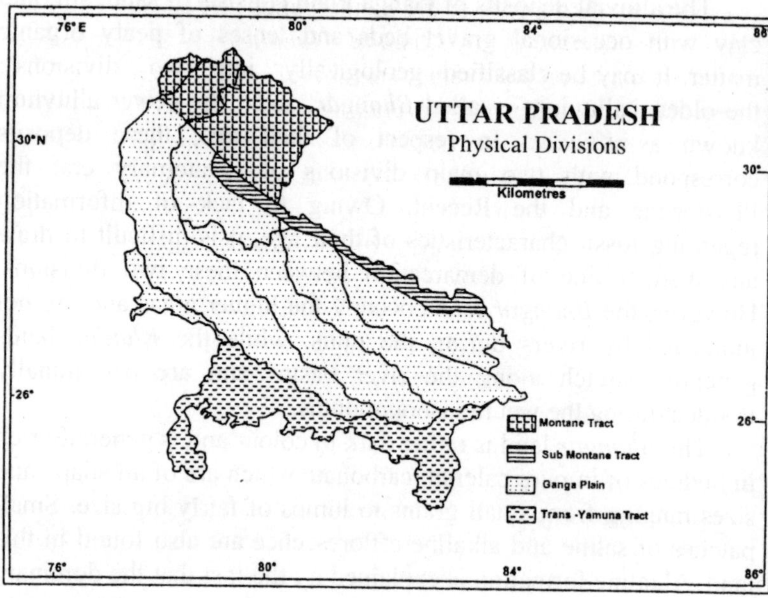

Fig. 3.1

The Montane Tract

The slope of the state is from northwest to southeast. The topography of the area is very rugged and highly dissected. It constitutes around 16 per cent of the total area of the state. Topographically, it can be divided into three zones:

(a) Greater Himalaya.
(b) Lesser Himalaya or Kumaon Himalaya.

(c) Sub-Himalaya or Siwalik.

(a) *Greater Himalaya :* The Greater Himalaya is northern most zone with an average height of 6000 metres and above. It consist of four main peaks, which are source of glaciers, i.e. Nandadevi (7817m), Kamet (7756m), Badrinath (7138m) and Trisul (7120m). These snowy peaks are source of major perennial rivers of state. The headwater of Ganga, i.e. Bhagirathi and Alaknanda, originate from the opposite of the Chaukhaba peak, while Yamuna has its source in Yamunotri Glacier lying on the south western slopes of the Bandarpunch peak.

(b) *Lesser Himalaya or Kumaon Himalaya :* The lesser Himalaya has an average height of 3000 metres with width varying from 80 to 100 kms. It comprises of various ridges and deep valleys. Some famous hill stations lie in this zone, viz. Mussoorie, Nainital, Ranikhet, Almora, Chakrata, Landsowne etc.

(c) *Sub-Himalaya or Siwalik :* The Siwalik is the outer range of Himalayan system. It constitutes small hills whose height varies between 300-600 metres. They have steep scarps on southern slopes, whereas they descend gently to the Duns in the north, the width of which is upto 24 km. Some important valleys are Dehradun, Kot Dun, Patli Dun, Kothri Dun, etc.

The Sub-montane Tract

This is situated in foothills of Himalayas. It consists of two parallel running tracts, i.e. (a) Bhangar; and (b) Terai

(a) *Bhangar :* It extends upto 30 km in the west and narrows towards east. It is just below Himalayas. This tract has little surface drainage.

(b) *Terai :* It is low marshy area with tall grasses and scrubs. Malaria is a common epidemic in this area. The rainfall is heavy and streams are numerous.

The Ganga Plains

The Ganga Plain covers nearly 50 per cent of the state. It can be divided into five regions:

(a) Ganga-Yamuna Doab.
(b) Ganga-Gomati Interfluve.
(c) Gomati-Ghaghara Interfluve.
(d) Trans-Ghaghara Plain.
(e) Rohilkhand Tract.

(a) *The Ganga-Yamuna Doab :* Covering an area of 58,400 sq. km., the Ganga Yamuna Doab has 832 km of length and 104 km of width. The general characteristics of this area is homogenous. The region is very fertile and the density of population is very high. It contains both Khadar and Bhangar lands. Khadar is a new alluvium closer to flood plain areas and is renewed almost every year through floods. Bhangar lies in comparatively higher lands.
(b) *The Ganga-Gomati Interfluve :* It is less fertile than the Ganga-Yamuna doab. The river Gomati flows in a sinuous course and causes water logging in rainy season. It is a perennial river, which is used for irrigation purposes.
(c) *The Gomati-Ghaghara Interfluve :* It is comparatively less fertile because it brings lot of sand in the plain as it descends from the mountains. Agriculture in this area is mostly rainfed. Therefore, overall agricultural production is low.
(d) *The Trans-Ghaghara Plain :* It is famous for producing rice and sugarcane. Bhat is a distinct type of soil found in this area.
(e) *The Rohilkhand Tract :* It includes upper regions of Ganga-Gomati doab. The soil is poor and productivity is moderate.

The Upland Regions

It covers the areas of Jhansi, Jalaun, Lalitpur, Hamirpur, Banda, Mirzapur, Sonbhadra and southern part of Allahabad district. It is rugged plateau with slopes towards north-east. It has infertile soil. The rainfall is low and variable.

Climate

The state experiences tropical monsoon climate with the exception of temperate climate prevailing in Himalayan region. With the reversal of the prevailing winds taking place regularly twice in a year, there are two monsoon seasons: the southwest monsoon season and northeast monsoon season. The former, extending from mid-June to October, is influenced by humid winds of oceanic origin, and is characterised by cloudy weather, high relative humidity and heavy rainfall, while the latter is distinguished by dry winds of continental origin, extremes of temperature, clear sky and low humidity. The two monsoons closely correspond with Kharif and Rabi agricultural seasons in the state respectively. However, on the basis of temperature and precipitation, the year could be divided into following seasons:

(a) The Hot Weather Season (March – mid-June)
(b) The Season of Rains (Mid-June – October)
(c) The Cold Weather Season (November – February)

The Hot Weather Season

This season begins in March and continues till mid-June. With abrupt rise in temperature, the atmospheric pressure and relative humidity fall. The mean monthly temperature varies between 21° and 26°C in plain region, whereas the mean maximum temperature varies between 7.5 and 12.5°C, and 34° and 39°C respectively. May is the hottest month in the plain with mean minimum and mean maximum temperature ranging between 18° and 23°C, and 42.6° and 45.6°C respectively. Usually the days are hot and nights are warm. The rainfall in this season is sporadic and frequently repeated about the same hours day after day in succession (Blanford, 1886). This little rainfall gives temporary relief from the intense heat of the day, and is quite helpful in preparation of fields for sowing of kharif crops but the violent winds accompanying the rain cause immense damage to the mangoes on trees.

The Season of Rains

The monsoon normally bursts in the middle of June and lasts till October. The oceanic currents bring a fall in temperature and upward trend in humidity. As a result the air becomes cool and pleasant. The air is saturated with vapour, and thick masses of clouds cover the sky. The relative humidity goes upto 90 per cent. July and August are the rainiest months of the year, and more than 50 per cent of annual rainfall is received during these months. Rainfall normally slackens and rainless intervals become longer in September but humidity remains high. And this, accompanied with cloudy weather makes the heat intolerable. Monsoon starts retreating in October, and very little rainfall, but quite useful for the rabi crops and for the maturity of late rice, is received in this month. The rainfall in the state (both monthly and annual) is highly variable ranging between 8 and 20 per cent, and it is in inreverse relationship with the amount of rainfall. It is assumed that places with a rainfall variability of 12 per cent or more, are liable to occurrence of famine (Blanford, 1886), and in this respect most of the areas of state are susceptible to famine. The lowest percentage (20 per cent) of variability is in north-western part of

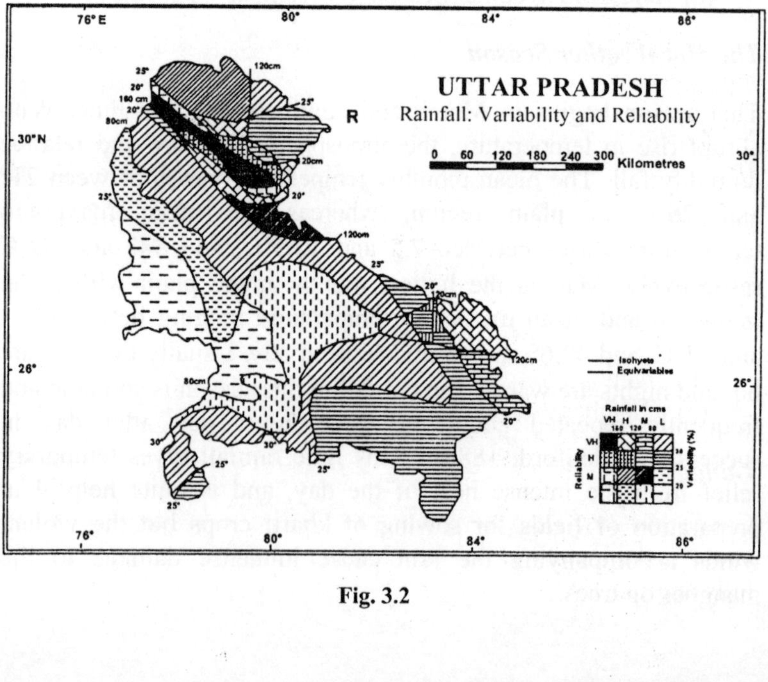

Fig. 3.2

the state where amount of rainfall is more than 120 cm. The other region, with similar variability condition, is the region of hilly districts with exception of extreme northern part, where variability is more than 25 per cent. As we move from east and southeast towards the west and northwest, the variability of rainfall increases, and consequently reliability decreases (Fig.3.2).

The Cold Weather Season

With the retreat of southwest monsoon by the end of October, the state comes under a high-pressure belt developed due to considerable fall in temperature. The direction of prevailing wind is eastward owing to pressure distribution and the influence exerted by Himalayan relief. During the day clear sky permits free insulation, while in the night, there is rapid radiation. With the result nights are cool and days are comparatively warm. The mean minimum temperature in November ranges between 5°-10°C, while mean maximum temperature varies from 25°-27°C. The temperature continues to decline gradually, and the month of January records the lowest temperature condition accompanied by mist, fog and frost. In February temperature starts increasing. During the period extending from December to February and sometimes even in March, a few depressions accompanied by moderate rainfall pass through the state. This small amount of rainfall is very beneficial to the winter crops because it comes at the time of the flowering of plants.

Drainage System

Drainage generally follows the slope and is closely linked with physiography. The state has basically following three major river systems (Fig.3.3).

(a) Ganga river system,
(b) Yamuna river system,
(c) Ghaghara river system.

Ganga river system

Ganga rises in Gangotri glaciers in Himalayas at an elevation of about 7,010 metres above sea level in the district of Uttarkashi. In hilly region, there are numerous tributaries, which are known by different names. However, Alaknanda and Bhagirathi, after joining at Devprayag are named as Ganga in their downward course. It is joined by many tributaries after Devprayag. The main tributaries of the river Ganga are Yamuna, Ramganga, Gangotri in Uttar Pradesh. Ram Ganga originates from the Himalaya and joins river Ganga near Kannauj. Gomati and its main tributary Sai runs almost parallel to Ganga. Sai joins Gomati only a few kilometres before it merges with Ganga. There are many other small tributaries flowing in the central part of the state.

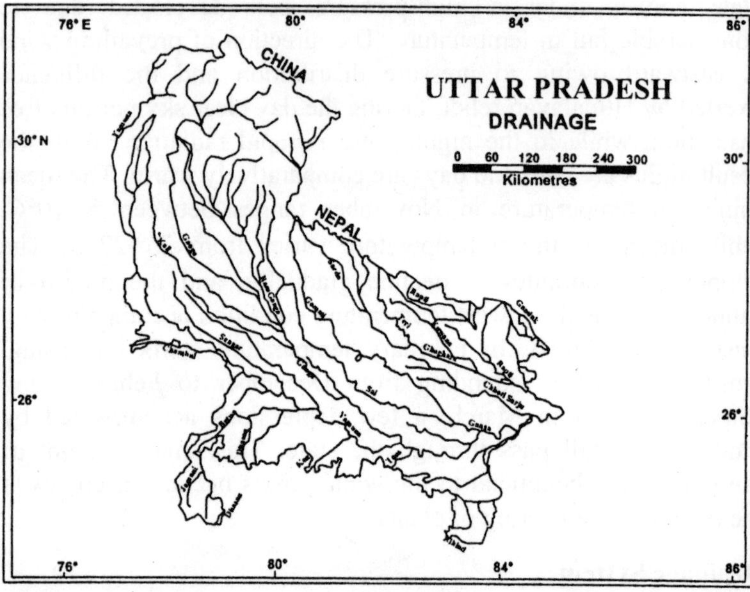

Fig. 3.3

Yamuna river system

Yamuna originates from Yamunotri Glaciers and runs parallel to Ganga and joins it at Allahabad. It is joined by small tributaries namely, Karos, Saugar and Rind on its left bank and by Chambal, Betwa, Son, Ken on its right bank.

Ghaghara river system

This river system flowing in the tortuous course drains the southern part of the state. Ghaghara enters from Nepal and runs parallel to Ganga and joins it beyond Ballia district. Its main tributaries are Rapti, Sarju, Kuwana and Gandak. This river causes floods in monsoon period.

SOILS

In *1983 National Bureau of Soil Survey and Landuse Planning (I.C.A.R.)* has classified soils of Uttar Pradesh into 11 major classes and 27 sub-order associations. Similarly, there are several other government organizations that have classified the soils of U.P. on the basis of their colour, texture, level of land and availability of water. However, based on information from settlement reports, gazetteers, assessment reports and revenue records, soils have been classified into following 7 categories in this study by taking into consideration the colour, texture, availability of water, level of land and its location with reference to settlement sites :

(a) Hill Soils,
(b) Bhabar Soils,
(c) Terai Soils,
(d) Alluvial Soils,
(e) Vindhyan Soils,
(f) Bundelkhand Soils,
(g) Aravalli Soils.

Hill Soils

This group of soil is found in 8 districts of Uttar Pradesh, i.e. Uttarkashi, Chamoli, Pauri Garhwal, Tehri Garhwal, Almora, Dehradun, Pithoragarh and Nainital districts. The normal reaction in these soils predominates between 59 and 66 per cent in the former three districts (Malhotra, 1972). Alkaline, organic carbon and potash is variedly distributed in different districts, e.g. Alkaline soil is found only in Pithoragarh.

Bhabar Soils

Rivers carry alluvial from hills and deposit it just in the foothills. This is called Bhabar soil. This is a fertile soil. It is found in the districts of Dehradun, Saharanpur, Bijnor, Garhwal and Nainital. These soils are dark in colour and moderately alkaline in reaction due to the shortage of moisture. Hence, the soil is unproductive in spite of having rich plant nutrients. Inferior crops like maize, small millets etc. are grown here.

Terai Soils

It is a stretch of soil found from Dehradun in northwest to Deoria in northeast. It covers 1.68 million hectares of land. It can be divided into: (i) Northwestern Terai and (ii) Northeastern Terai. The former extends from Dehradun to Kheri district, while the latter runs between Bahraich and Deoria districts. It remains saturated during monsoon months and continue to be moist during succeeding winter due to very high level of underground water. The soils in eastern and western tract are fertile with good reserves of plant nutrients. Potash content is high in Saharanpur and calcium rich soil, called *Bhat*, is found in parts of northeastern Terai.

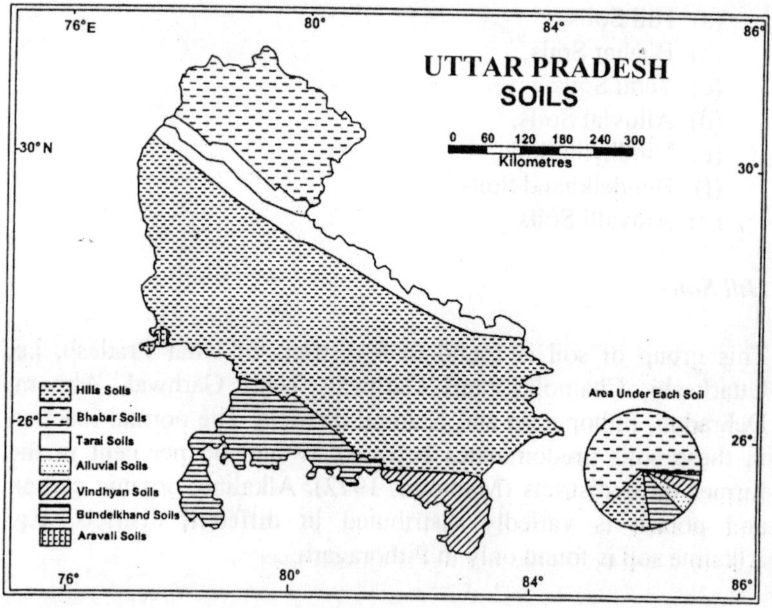

Fig. 3.4

Alluvial Soils

It is extensively found in the central, eastern, western and southern parts of the state. They cover 62 per cent of the total area of the state. The river Ganga forms the rich alluvium soil. Even Yamuna and its tributaries also contribute to the formation of alluvial soil of Ganga. It is different from that of Yamuna due to difference in parent material. These differences originate from the region from where the two rivers flow. The river Ganga flows from Himalayan rocks, while river Yamuna moves through basaltic rocks. In the western districts soil is generally alkaline. In Trans-Ghaghara plain the concentration of salt is low and potash level is moderate. These soils are very productive and fertile. Most of the agriculture in Uttar Pradesh is carried out in this region. Modernization of agriculture has also taken place in this regions. High yielding varieties of seeds, chemical fertilizers etc. are used in this area to increase the productivity of soil.

Vindhyan Soils

These soils are dark brown in colour, gravelly to sand loam in texture and poor in plant nutrients. These soils are found along river Ganga in districts of Varanasi, Allahabad and Mirzapur. The Vindhyan lowland soils are alluvial in character and are most fertile. It is mainly devoted to rice cultivation while the upland soil is found under excessive flooding and is poor in plant nutrient.

Bundelkhand Soils

These soils are called plateau soils and have their origin from Vindhyan rocks of Deccan-trap. It is a non-alluvial soil found in northwest of Yamuna in the district of Jhansi, Etawah, Hamirpur and Banda. On the basis of their colour, texture, parent material

Table 3.1 : Soil Groups in Uttar Pradesh

S. No	*Soil Group*	*Area in hectare*	*%age to total*
1.	Hill Soils	4217440	14.33
2.	Bhabar Soils	590510	2.00
3.	Terai Soils	1680740	5.73
4.	Alluvial Soils	18185300	61.78
5.	Vindhyan Soils	1501290	5.10
6.	Bundelkhand Soils	3192440	10.85
7.	Aravalli Soils	63290	0.21
	Total	**29437010**	**100.00**

and crops grown, the soil can be divided into four groups, i.e. Bundelkhand grained reddish brown, Bundelkhand course grained grey to greyish brown, Bundelkhand black clayey loam and Bundelkhand clayey black soils.

Aravalli Soils

The soil is found in northwestern part of Agra. They are course and gravel or sandy loam. They occupy 0.21 per cent of the total area of the state. These soils are poor and are devoted to cultivation of inferior crops.

ECONOMIC SETTING

Uttar Pradesh has essentially agricultural based economy. Around 80 per cent of the total population of the state is involved in agriculture, directly or indirectly. Besides agriculture, there are other sources of income too but in this section major emphasis is given to land use, especially agricultural land use. A statistical account of general land use in the state is given in Table 3.2.

Table 3.2 : Pattern of Land Use

S. No.	*Category*	*Area*	*% age to total*
1	Forest	5154357	17.29
2	Land N.A. for Cultivation	3504221	11.76
3	Other Uncultivated Land excluding Fallow Land	1871474	6.28
4	Fallow Land	2007696	6.73
5	Net Sown Area	17258878	57.94
	Total	**29796626**	**100.00**

Table 3.2 shows that forest occupies 17.29 per cent of the total area of the state which is less than the national average. It was 16.97 per cent in 1971. Due to various afforestation policies of the government and establishment of various national parks and wild life sanctuaries the situation has improved. Government has made strict laws against deforestation. The land not available for cultivation occupied around 12 per cent of the total area. Out of this, substantial percentage is covered by settlements. Other uncultivated land and fallow land occupy almost equal percentage of the total area but the net sown area covers about 58 per cent of

the total which indicates the suitability of the state for agricultural activities (Fig. 3.5).

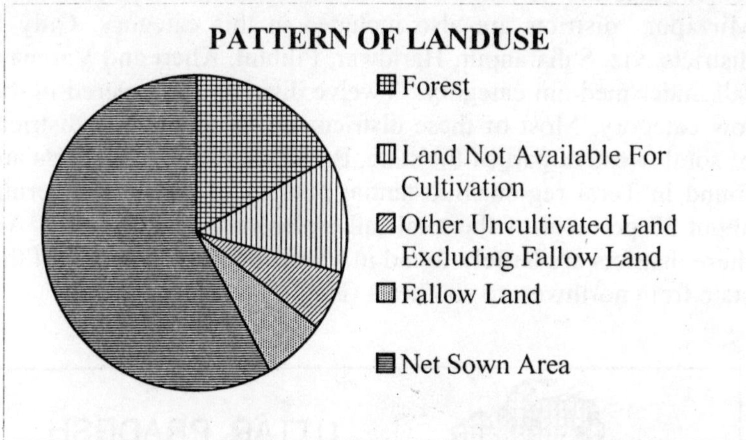

Fig. 3.5

The preceding analysis represents the aggregate picture of landuse in the state but there are a lot of spatial variations in all the categories of landuse. Hence, a brief description of spatial variations in all the five categories of landuse is given here.

Forest

Although forests cover about 17 per cent of the total area of the state but its percentage strength varies from zero per cent in at least 7 districts of central eastern Uttar Pradesh to 60 per cent in the district of Uttrakhand. Based on this range, the state is divided into four regions (Table 3.3).

Table 3.3 : Forest Cover to Total Area of the Districts

Category	*Range in %*	*No. of Districts*	*%age to total*
High	>25	10	15.88
Medium	15-25	5	7.93
Low	5-15	12	19.04
Very Low	<5	36	57.15
Total		**63**	**100.00**

Table 3.3 shows that 10 districts covering about 16 per cent of the total districts have more than 25 per cent of their total area

under forest. But a closer scrutiny of the master table shows that 9 out of 10 districts have more than half of their total area under forest. Besides 8 districts of Uttrakhand, Sonbhadra and Mirzapur districts are also included in this category. Only 5 districts, viz. Saharanpur, Haridwar, Pilibhit, Kheri and Varanasi fall under medium category. Twelve districts are covered in the low category. Most of these districts are the peripheral districts of south western part of the state. Besides these, five districts are found in Terai region. Substantial number of districts covering about 57 per cent of the total fall under very low category. All these districts are largely found in a wide belt in the centre of the state from northwest to southeast (Fig.3.6).

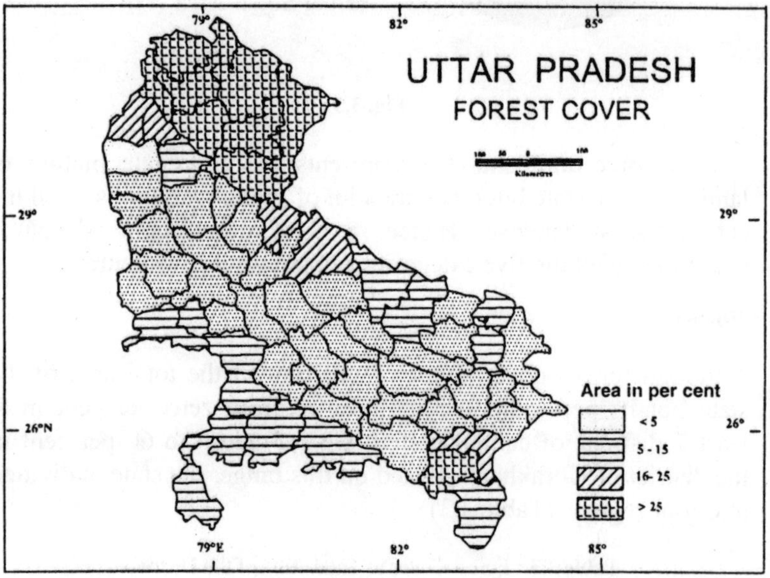

Fig. 3.6

Area Not Available for Cultivation

This category comprises of two sub-categories, i.e. area under non-agricultural uses, and barren and uncultivable land. It occupies 11.76 per cent of the total area of the state. In 1971 it was

11.30 per cent. The small rise in this category is due to urbanization. Area under non-agricultural uses has increased. Many houses, industries, and road networks have occupied this space.

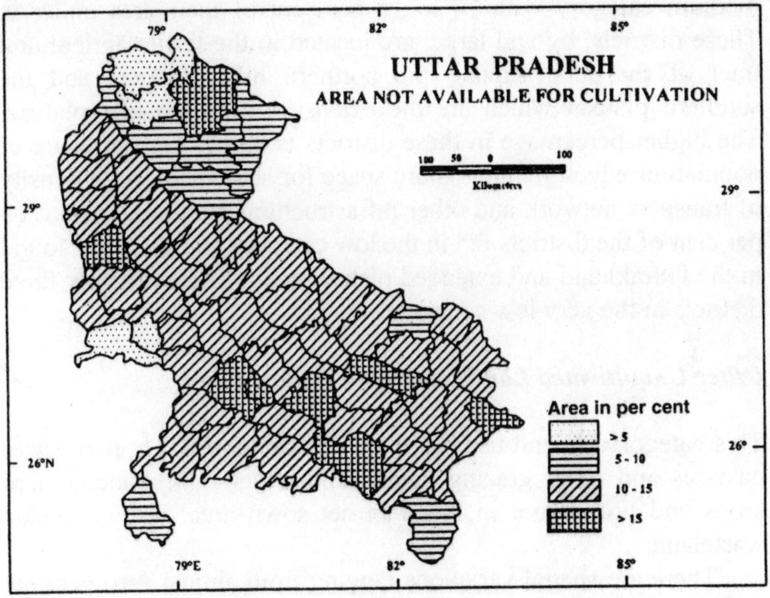

Fig. 3.7

The spatial pattern of distribution of this category is also varied (Fig.3.7). It ranges from almost one per cent to about 22 per cent of the total area of the district. Hence, on the basis of the percentage range the state has been divided into four categories (Table 3.4).

Table 3.4 : Area Not Available for Cultivation

Category	*Range in %*	*No. of Districts*	*%age to Total*
High	>15	8	12.70
Medium	10-15	44	69.84
Low	5-10	8	12.70
Very Low	<5	3	4.76
Total		**63**	**100.00**

It is evident from Table 3.4 that 8 districts covering about 13 per cent of the total districts fall in the high category with more than 15 per cent of their total area under this type of land. These districts are widely scattered all over the state. Substantial number of districts covering about 70 per cent of the total belong to medium category with 10 to 15 per cent of their area under it. These districts, by and large, are located in the fertile agricultural tract of the state leaving the northern hilly districts and the southern plateau which are the extension of peninsular plateau. The higher percentage in these districts is due to high pressure of population which requires more space for settlement, high density of transport network and other infrastructural facilities. About 13 per cent of the districts fall in the low category and these are found in the Uttrakhand and extended plateau area. There are only three districts in the very low category.

Other Uncultivated Land Excluding Fallow Land

This category of land use has three sub-categories, i.e. permanent pastures and other grazing lands; land under miscellaneous tree crops and groves not included in net sown area; and cultivable wasteland.

There are spatial variations ranging from almost zero per cent in Rampur district to 28 per cent in Pithoragarh (Fig.3.8). Hence, on the basis of the percentage range the districts have been grouped into four categories (Table 3.5).

Table 3.5 : Uttar Pradesh : Other Uncultivated Land Except Fallow Land

Category	*Range in %*	*No. of Districts*	*%age to total*
High	>6	18	28.58
Medium	4-6	12	19.04
Low	2-4	25	39.68
Very Low	<2	8	12.70
Total		**63**	**100.00**

It is obvious from Table 3.5 that about 29 per cent districts fall under high category with more than 6 per cent of their total area under this category. However, there are five districts, viz. Bijnor, Garhwal, Lalitpur, Almora and Pithoragarh where it covers more than 20 per cent of their total area, while in Jhansi, Rae Bareli and

Chamoli it covers about one–tenth of the total area. About one-fifth of the districts fall in the medium category and they are scattered all over the state. Almost two-fifths of the districts fall under low category with 2-4 per cent of their total area under this category. The distribution pattern of these districts is also uneven. Only 8 districts fall under very low category with less than 2 per cent of their total area. These districts also do not form contiguous belt.

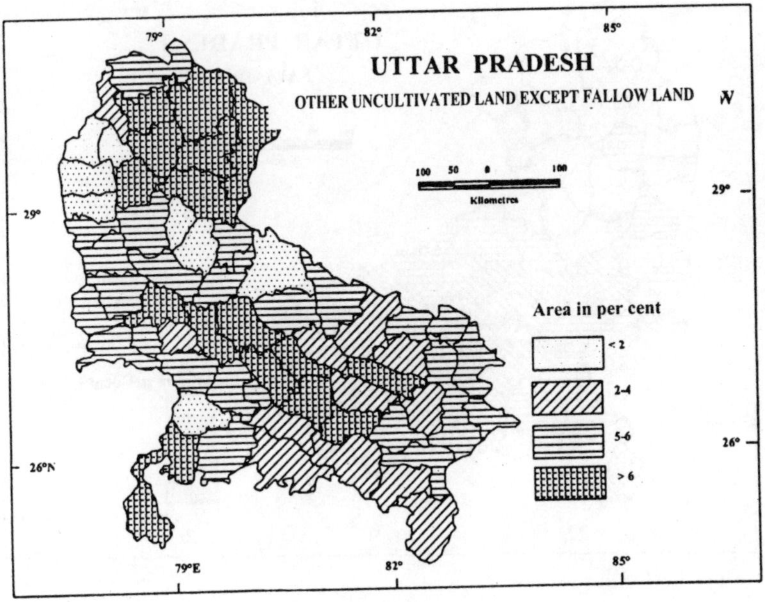

Fig. 3.8

Fallow Land

This category comprises of two sub-categories, i.e. fallow land other than current fallows and current fallow land. About 7 per cent of the total area of the state is fallow land. Out of this 55 per cent is current fallow. The percentage strength of fallow land also varies from almost zero per cent in Chamoli district to 18 per cent in Lucknow (Fig.3.9). On the basis of their percentage range the districts have been divided into four categories (Table3.6).

Table 3.6 : Fallow Land

Category	*Range in %*	*No. of Districts*	*%age to total*
High	>6	18	28.58
Medium	4-6	12	19.04
Low	2-4	25	39.68
Very Low	<2	8	12.70
Total		**63**	**100.00**

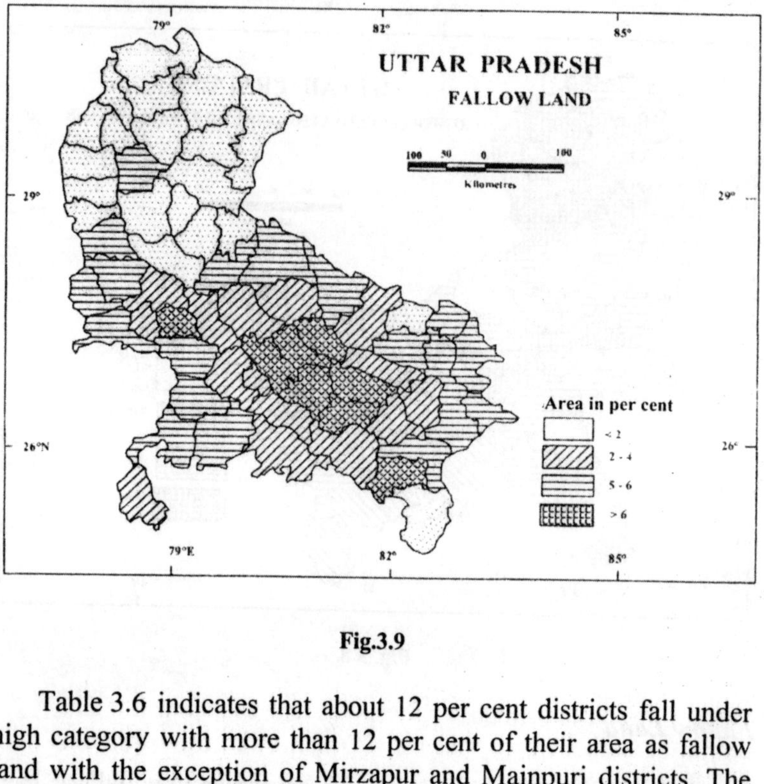

Fig.3.9

Table 3.6 indicates that about 12 per cent districts fall under high category with more than 12 per cent of their area as fallow land with the exception of Mirzapur and Mainpuri districts. The remaining 6 districts form a compact patch in the heart of the state around its capital. Out of 8 districts of this category 5 districts have more than 15 per cent of their area under fallow. More than 27 per cent districts belong to medium category. These districts are quite unevenly distributed. About one-third districts fall under low category each. These districts are mainly found in the areas with poor soil.

Net Sown Area

This is the category of land, which is used for cultivating various kinds of crops. It covers about 18 million hectares or about 57 per cent of the total area of the state. But the scrutiny of the master table shows that there is a lot of variation in the areal strength of this category ranging from about 4 per cent in Uttrakhand to about 83 per cent in Siddharthnagar. However, based on percentage strength districts have been put into 4 categories (Table 3.7).

Table 3.7 : Net Sown Area

Category	*Range in %*	*No. of Districts*	*%age to total*
High	>60	50	79.37
Medium	40-60	3	4.76
Low	20-40	3	4.76
Very Low	<20	7	11.11
Total		**63**	**100.00**

Table 3.7 shows that around 79 per cent of the districts have more than 60 per cent of their area as agricultural land. Out of this 5 districts, viz. Bareilly, Mathura, Moradabad, Rampur and Siddharthnagar have more than 80 per cent of their area under this category, while 26 districts have 70 to 80 per cent of their area as agricultural land. The remaining 19 districts have about 60 to 70 per cent of their total area under this category. The medium and low categories cover about 5 per cent each of the total districts, while low category accounts more than one-tenth of the total districts. All these three categories are widely scattered all over the state specially in the hilly districts of Uttrakhand (Fig.3.10).

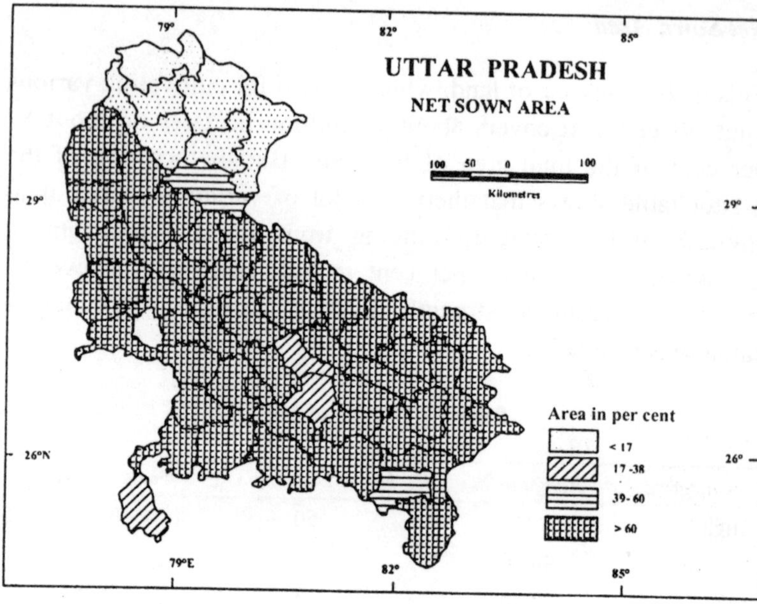

Fig. 3.10

CROPPING PATTERN

The cropping pattern of Uttar Pradesh is extremely varied. Various crops are grown in the state. It has both Kharif and Rabi seasons in its agricultural year. The Kharif crops are called the *summer crops* and Rabi crops are known as *winter crops*. The principal Kharif crops are rice, maize, jowar, bajra, sugarcane and groundnut. The major Rabi crops are wheat, lentil, barley, gram, peas and potatoes. It can be noticed that all the crops are not grown in all the areas. Due to varied climatic and physiographic factors, the agriculture in the state of Uttar Pradesh is complex. The cropping pattern is also influenced by various socio-economic factors. Irrigation is one of the major factor responsible for cropping pattern in Uttar Pradesh. However, according to agricultural seasons, a brief account of cropping pattern is given here.

Cropping Pattern in Kharif Season

Kharif is the major agricultural season in the state. Variety of crops such as rice, jowar, bajra, maize, sugarcane etc. are grown in this season (Fig.3.11). Almost all the Kharif crops are grown without irrigation except sugarcane and new variety of rice. The sowing of Kharif crops starts with the onset of monsoon generally in the second week of June, while harvesting takes place in September-October.

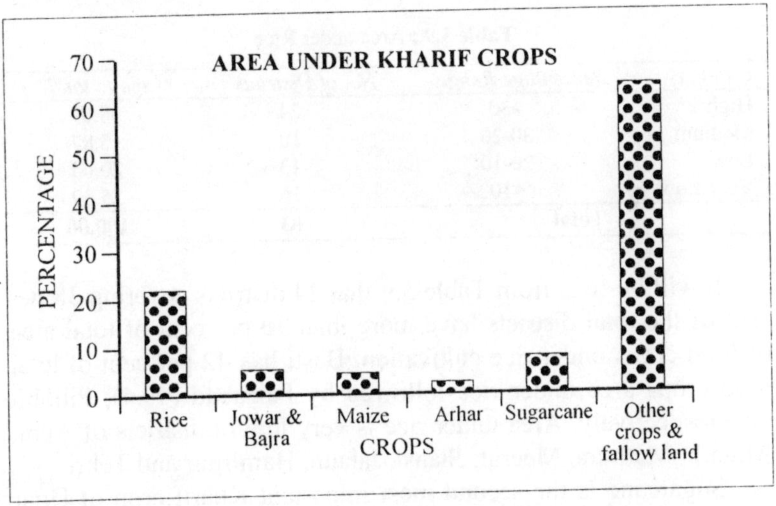

Fig. 3.11

It can be seen from Table 3.8 that rice occupies around 20 per cent of total cropped area. It is followed by sugarcane, jowar and bajra, maize and *arhar* respectively. Remaining land is either under other crops or is left fallow.

Table 3.8 : Area under Principal Kharif Crops

Crops	*Area ('000)*	*%age to total*
Rice	5617	20.29
Jowar & Bajra	1312	4.74
Maize	1095	3.96
Arhar	502	1.81
Sugarcane	1856	6.70
Other crops & fallow land	17299	62.49
Total	**27681**	**100.00**

Rice is the major kharif crop grown in this area. Area under rice cultivation has shown a tremendous increase after 1966-67 because of improvement in agricultural infrastructure and introduction of new variety of seeds. For example, in 1966-67 the areal strength of rice was 4.31 m.ha. which has increased to 5.60 m.ha. in 1990-91. Similarly production and yield have also shown a rising trend. However, according to the percentage coverage of rice, the districts have been grouped into four categories (Table 3.9).

Table 3.9 : Area under Rice

Category	*Percentage Range*	*No. of Districts*	*%age to total*
High	>30	24	38.09
Medium	30-20	10	15.87
Low	20-10	13	20.65
Very Low	<10	16	25.39
	Total	**63**	**100.00**

It will be seen from Table 3.9 that 24 districts covering 38 per cent of the total districts have more than 30 per cent of total area of food crops under rice cultivation. Basti has 42 per cent of total food crops area under rice followed by Faizabad (40.4), Pilibhit (40) respectively. Area under rice is very low in districts of Agra, Aligarh, Mathura, Meerut, Jhansi, Jalaun, Hamirpur and Tehri.

Sugarcane is the second most important Kharif crop of Uttar Pradesh. It occupies about 1.9 million hectares of area. It was 1.20 million hectares in 1980-81. The yield of sugarcane has also gone up. It is an important cash crop of farmers in this area. However, on the basis of the percentage coverage of sugarcane, the districts have been grouped into 4 categories (Table 3.10).

Table 3.10 : Area under Sugarcane

Category	*Percentage Range*	*No. of Districts*	*%age to total*
High	>30	3	4.70
Medium	30-20	2	3.17
Low	20-10	6	9.05
Very Low	<10	52	82.53
	Total	**63**	**100.00**

From Table 3.10 it will be seen that 82.53 per cent, i.e. 52 districts covering about 82 per cent of the total districts have less than 10 per cent of their total food crops area under sugarcane cultivation. Three districts, i.e. Saharanpur, Meerut and Bijnor have more than 30 per cent of their food crops area under sugarcane cultivation. Besides these, there are several other crops grown in the state.

Cropping Pattern in Rabi Season

Rabi is the second important agricultural season in the state. Wheat, barley, gram and pulses are the important crops of Rabi season (Fig.3.12).

AREA UNDER RABI CROPS

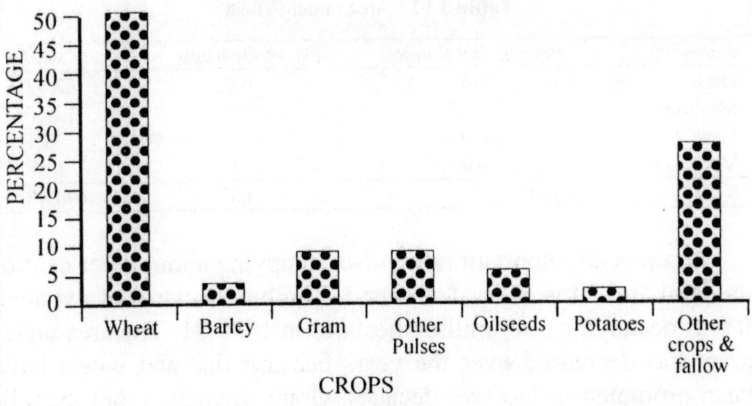

Fig. 3.12

A statistical account of the areal coverage of major rabi crops is given in Table 3.11.

Table 3.11 : Area under Rabi Crops

Crops	*Area (in '000 hectare)*	*%age to total*
Wheat	8568	49.53
Barley	470	2.72
Gram	1304	7.54
Other Pulses	1346	7.78
Oilseeds	717	4.14
Potatoes	336	1.94
Other crops & fallow	45558	26.35
Total	**17299**	**100.00**

Wheat is the most dominant crop of this season. It is cultivated over 8.57 million hectares of land. It had covered 7.89 million hectares in 1980-81. It accounts for 49.53 per cent of the total cropped area of rabi season. It has shown a significant increase in production and yield over last two decades. However, based on the areal coverage of the wheat, the districts have been classified into four categories (Table 3.12). Table 3.12 shows that around 82.53 per cent of districts, i.e. 52 districts have more than 30 per cent of their food crop area under wheat. Wheat is predominantly grown in Unnao, Rae Bareli, Basti, Mau, Gorakhpur, Shahjahanpur, Badaun etc. Mathura has around 60 per cent of its total food crop area under wheat cultivation. In Muzaffarnagar only 15 per cent of area under food crop is used for wheat cultivation.

Table 3.12 : Area under Wheat

Category	*Percentage Range*	*No. of Districts*	*% to total*
High	>30	52	82.53
Medium	30-20	8	12.69
Low	20-10	2	3.1
Very Low	<10	1	1.58
	Total	**63**	**100.00**

Gram is an important rabi pulse occupying about 8 per cent of the total area. It is cultivated over 1.3 million hectares of the area. It was occupying 1.41 million hectares in 1980-81. The area under gram has decreased over the years because rice and wheat have been promoted in last two decades. Gram occupies more than 20 per cent of the total food crop area in Jhansi, Jalaun and Banda.

Table 3.13 : Area under Gram

Category	*Percentage Range*	*No. of Districts*	*% to total*
High	>20	4	6.34
Medium	20-15	1	1.58
Low	15-10	3	4.76
Very Low	<10	55	87.30
	Total	**63**	**100.00**

About 87 per cent of the districts have devoted less than 10 per cent of food crop area to the cultivation of gram (Table 3.13). Besides these, there are several other rabi crops grown in the state.

SOCIAL SETTING

Uttar Pradesh is one of the most densely populated state of India. It has a total population of 138,760,417 persons with a density of 473 persons/sq. km (1991). It was 377 persons per sq. km. in 1981. In terms of density of population Uttar Pradesh comes after West Bengal (767), Kerala (749) and Bihar (497). The spatial distribution of density of population is shown in Fig.3.13.

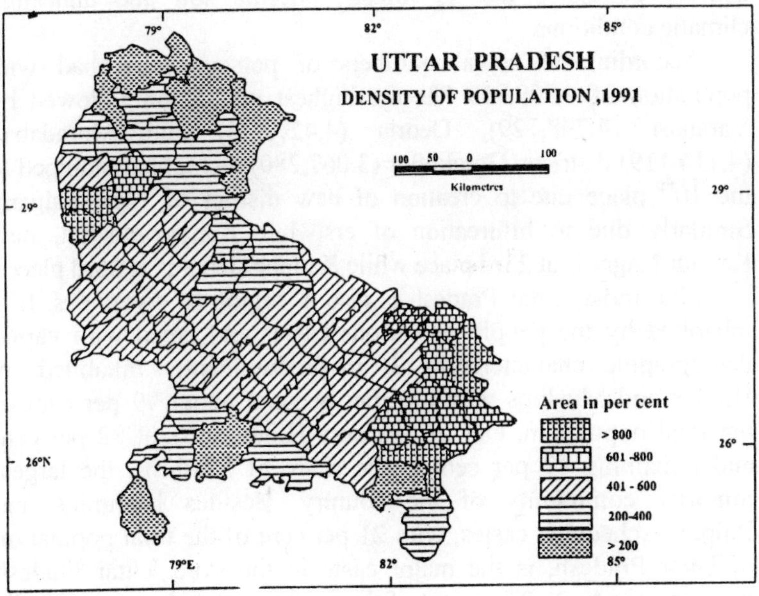

Fig. 3.13

Fig. 3.13 depicts that density of population is high in plain areas than in mountainous regions. Eastern part of the state adjoining Bihar has high density of population ranging between 600 to more than 800 persons per sq. km. Similarly the western Uttar Pradesh also has scattered districts of high density of population. Density of population is low in southern and northern parts of UP adjoining Madhya Pradesh and Himachal Pradesh respectively. The lowest density of the state is witnessed in Bundelkhand Plateau, Mirzapur Uplands and Himalayan region. At tehsil level, Kanpur tehsil has highest density of population, i.e. 2271 persons per sq. km. followed by Agra and Lucknow respectively. Joshimath tehsil of Chamoli has the lowest density of population, i.e. around 13 persons per sq. km. It is found that density of population in Uttar Pradesh corresponds to its physical setting. Plain areas where agriculture is mostly practiced have more density of population than the uplands. The central part of the state shows normal distribution of population because of limited irrigation facilities and inadequate and variable rainfall. The Terai region at the foothills of Himalayas is not densely populated due to forests, infertile soil and unhealthy climatic conditions.

According to actual numbers of persons Allahabad with population of 4,909,919 has the highest population followed by Varanasi (4,798,729), Deoria (4,427,345) and Moradabad (4,114,119) districts. Gorakhpur (3,067,280) district has slumped to the 10th place due to creation of new district of Maharajganj, Similarly due to bifurcation of erstwhile Kanpur district, new Kanpur Nagar is at 23rd place while Kanpur Dehat is at 36rd place.

Like India, Uttar Pradesh is also a region of diversities. It is inhabited by the people of various castes and creed with varied demographic characteristics. It is predominantly inhabited by Hindus and Muslims who together account about 99 per cent of the total population. Out of this only Hindu account 82 per cent and remaining 17 per cent is the share of Muslims, the largest minority community of the country. Besides Brahmins and Rajputs, scheduled castes, with 21 per cent of the total population of Uttar Pradesh, is the major caste in the state. Uttar Pradesh supports nearly 21.2 per cent of the total scheduled castes of India where the share of the scheduled castes population is only 3.49 per cent of the total population.

The spatial distribution of scheduled castes is quite uneven, and their percentage contribution to the total population of the districts ranges from as low as one per cent to as high as 35 per cent. The higher concentration with more than 26 per cent and above is found in a elongated belt running from Jhansi in south to Pilibhit in the north in the central part, two major patches in eastern part and one patch in extreme northeastern part of the state. The regions of moderate concentration have mostly emanated from high concentration zones and they cover almost whole eastern Uttar

Pradesh leaving few exceptions. The biggest chunk of low concentration region running from Chamoli in the north to Farrukhabad district in the south, lies in the central northern part of the state.

The scheduled caste population has a heterogeneous demographic character. Nearly 88 per cent of the total live in rural areas, while only 12 per cent belong to urban centres. The literacy level is very low, whereas the sex ratio is 884 among rural and 860 among urban population. Most of the scheduled caste population is engaged in labour.

According to the occupational structure the working population is divided into 4 major categories, i.e. cultivators, agricultural labourers, household industry and, other workers. All these categories add up to form main workers. Besides these there are marginal workers and non-workers. Main workers account for around 30 per cent of the total population of the state. Observing the spatial distribution of the main workers it can be seen that about 5.7 per cent, i.e. 36 districts, the population of main workers to total population is less than 30 per cent, while in only 4 districts it is more than 40 per cent. These 4 districts lie in extreme north. They are Uttarkashi, Chamoli, Pithoragarh and Tehri Garhwal.

Table 3.14 : Percentage Distribution of Main Workers

Category	*Percentage Range*	*No. of Districts*	*%age of total*
High	> 40	4	6.36
Medium	40-35	3	4.76
Low	35-30	20	31.74
Very low	<30	36	57.14
	Total	**63**	**100.00**

Among the main workers, cultivators accounting nearly 53 per cent of the total workers dominate the scene (Table 3.14). It is followed by the agricultural workers who account nearly one-fifth of the total workers. A close examination of data shows that majority of the cultivators are non-scheduled castes, while scheduled caste take lion's share of agricultural workers. There are large number of workers amounting to nearly one-fourth of main workers who have not specified their occupation clearly or they are too many to be given as a category. Nearly 4 per cent people are engaged in household industry. The state is inhabited by the people of different castes. Brahmins, Rajputs and scheduled castes constitute the substantial percentage of the population of the state.

REFERENCES

Mohammad, N.,1992 : 'Pattern of Agricultural Landuse in Ghaghara-Rapti Doab' in Mohammad, N.(ed.), *New Dimensions in Agricultural Geography*, Vol.V., Concept Pub. Co. New Delhi.

Oldham, R.D. 1917: 'The Structure of Himalayas and Gangetic Plain', *Memoirs of the Geological Survey of India*, Vol. XLII, Pt. II, Calcutta.

Panse, V.G. and Singh, D., 1966: Promotion and Assessment of Technological Change in Indian Agriculture, *Indian Journal of Agricultural Economics*, Vol. XXI.

Rahudkar, W.P., 1962 : Farmer's Characteristic Associated with the Adoption and Diffusion of Improved Farm practices, *Indian Journal of Agricultural Economics,* Vol. XVII.

Rangaswamy, P., *et al.*,1972 : *India's Changing Farmers*, Allahabad.

Raychaudhari, S.P. *et al.* 1963: *Soils of India*, New Delhi.

Raychaudhari, S.P. and Mukerjee, S.K. 1947 : *Present Position of Soil Survey in India*, J.S.I.R.

Salve, R.S., 1966: 'Technological Change in Agricultural Development : Role of Irrigation and Cropping Pattern', *Indian Journal of Agricultural Economics*, Vol. XXI.

Shafi, M.,1960 : *Land Utilization in Eastern Uttar Pradesh,* Aligarh.

Shafi, M.,1984 : *Agricultural Productivity and Regional Imbalances,* Concept Publishing Co., New Delhi.

Shiva, V.,1991: *The Violence of Green Cultivation*, Mapusa, Goa.

Singh, J. and Dhillon, S.S., 1994: *Agricultural Geography*, Tata McGrow-Hill Pub. Co., New Delhi.

Singh, R.P., 1992: 'Concept of Landuse' in Mohammad, N.(ed.), *New Dimensions in Agricultural Geography*, Vol.IV., Concept Pub. Co. Delhi.

Sinha, A., 1982: *Caste System: Myths, Reality, Challenge*, New Delhi.

Spate, O.H.K. and Learmonth, A.T.A.,1967: *India and Pakistan*, London.

Subbiah, S. and Ahmad, A.,1980: Determinants of Agricultural Productivity in Tamil Nadu, India, '*Transaction of Institute of Indian Geographers*', No.1, Vol.II, pp.19-32.

Trewarth, G.T., 1962: *The Earth's Problem Climate*, London.

Wadia, D.N. and Auden, J.B. 1939: Geology and Structure of Northern India, *Memoirs of the Geological Survey of India*, Vol. LXXIII, Delhi.

Wadia, D.N., 1976: *Geology of India*, Tata McGraw Hill, New Delhi.

Weaver, J.C., 1954: Crop-Combination Regions in Middle-West, *The Geographical Review*, Vol. XLIV.

4

SOCIO-ECONOMIC STRUCTURE OF RESPONDENTS

PERSONAL AND HOUSEHOLD CHARACTERISTICS OF RESPONDENTS

Besides the physio-economic factors, the socio-cultural factors specially human psychology and behaviour play significant role in the process of socio-economic transformation. It affects the choice of occupation, adoption of innovation, exposure to mass media, level of religiosity, attitude to family welfare programme, education and job of the children, social mobility, status of political awareness and involvement, housing condition and so on. These are the manifestation of age, education, caste, family size, occupation, place of residence which are intrinsically related with one another. But there are a lot of variations among urban-rural, and scheduled castes and non-scheduled castes in these parameters. The basic aim of this chapter is, therefore, to assess the homogeneity and dissimilarities in the personal and family attributes of 1510 selected respondents of the study area with reference to the selected parameters.

Age Composition of Respondents

In the process of overall development in general and rural development in particular the age composition of population plays very significant role as it helps in adoptions of new ideas and practices which in turn bring economic benefits and prosperity. It has been observed that the younger generation is more receptive to various kinds of innovations, whereas at an advanced stage people find it difficult to change from age old practices, and they resist to adoption of innovations (Mohammad, 1978). With this view all the respondents have been classified into four categories on the basis of their age (Table 4.1).

Table 4.1 : Age Composition of All Respondents

Age Group	*Age Range*	*No. of Respondents*	*%age to total*
Young Age	<30 years	215	14.24
Lower Middle Age	30-39 years	397	26.29
Upper Middle Age	40-49 years	395	26.16
Old Age	50 & above years	503	33.31
Total		**1510**	**100.00**

Table 4.1 gives very interesting picture regarding the age composition of the respondents. Generally the number of respondents increases with increasing age which indicates that the elder people still dominate in the decision making process (Fig.4.1). Hence, they occupy about one-third of the total number of respondents. But the encouraging fact is that the middle aged respondents (both upper and lower) account more than 52 per cent of the respondents which shows that gradually the younger generation is coming up and actively participating in the decision making process of household affairs. About 15 per cent of younger generation participate in decision making process.

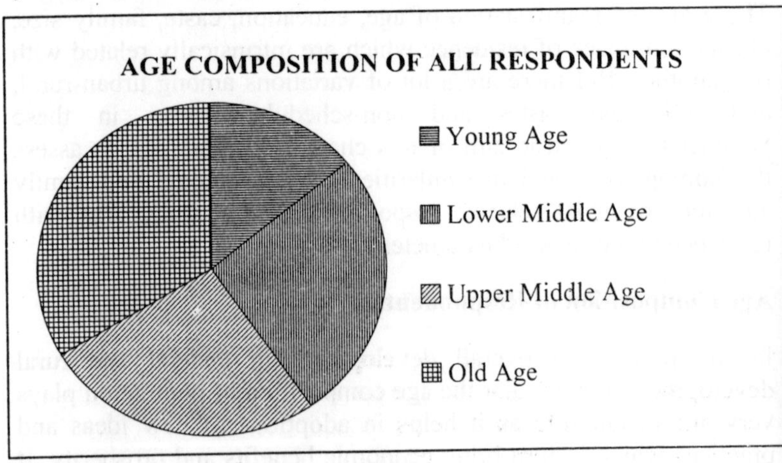

Fig. 4.1

However, the above analysis gives only aggregate picture of the involvement of respondents in the decision making process but there are a lot of variations among scheduled castes and non-scheduled castes, rural and urban scheduled castes, rural non-scheduled castes and urban non-scheduled castes which gets reflected in the age composition of these categories of respondents. Therefore, in the succeeding pages age composition of the respondents with reference to all these parameters have been discussed and analysed.

Age Composition of Scheduled Caste Respondents

The overall age composition of scheduled caste population is different from the general trend. Table 4.2 gives a statistical statement of the age composition of all scheduled caste respondents. It is obvious from Table 4.2 that nearly 13 per cent of the scheduled caste respondents belong to the age group of less than 30 years, whereas 302 respondents amounting to about 27 per cent of the total 1112 respondents belong to the lower middle age group. It is slightly less than the number of respondents belonging to upper middle age group. The contribution of the old age respondents is almost the same, viz. one-third of the respondents as in case of all respondents (Fig.4.2). The analysis of

AGE COMPOSITION OF ALL SCHEDULED CASTE RESPONDENTS

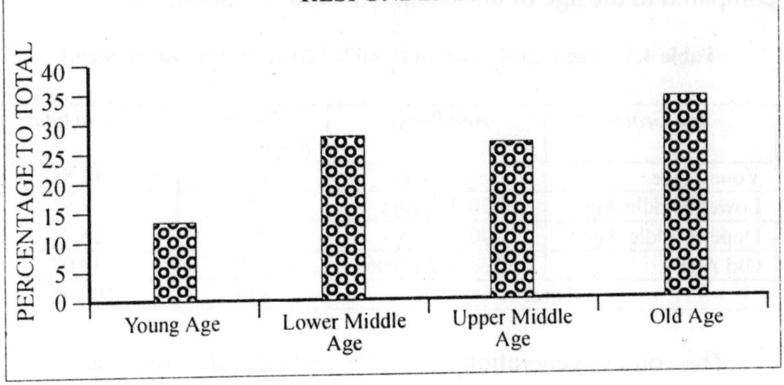

Fig. 4.2

Table 4.2 : Age Composition of All Scheduled Caste Respondents

Age Group	*Age Range*	*No. of Respondents*	*% age to total*
Young Age	<30 years	144	12.95
Lower Middle Age	30-39 years	302	27.16
Upper Middle Age	40-49 years	292	26.26
Old Age	50 & above years	374	33.63
Total		**1112**	**100.00**

this table indicates that although there is an overall upward movement of younger generation in the participation of decision making process in the household matters but it has not obtained the similar status of the overall population of the study area. Therefore, there is a need to encourage the younger generation not only to participate in the household activities but also to play a leading role in the process of decision making in the family affairs.

Age Composition of Rural Scheduled Caste Respondents

Table 4.2 represents the aggregate picture of the age composition of the total scheduled castes population but the status is quite different when we look into the age composition of the rural and urban scheduled caste respondents. Table 4.3 represents the statistical account of the age composition of the rural scheduled castes population, which indicates slightly different picture as compared to the age of all scheduled caste respondents.

Table 4.3 : Age Composition of Rural Scheduled Castes Respondents

Age Group	*Age Range*	*No. of Respondents*	*%age to total*
Young Age	<30 years	102	12.55
Lower Middle Age	30-39 years	225	27.67
Upper Middle Age	40-49 years	209	25.71
Old Age	50 & above years	277	34.07
Total		**813**	**100.00**

The older generation of rural scheduled castes accounts slightly more than one-third of the total 813 rural scheduled castes, while the younger generation of less than 30 years account about 12.6 per cent of the total rural scheduled castes. The comparative analysis of Tables 4.2 and 4.3 shows that in the rural areas the older generation still dominates in the decision making process on the family matters and the role of the younger generation is not very significant. A cursory glance at the master table and in depth scrutiny of the questionnaire shows that many of these young respondents do not take leading role in the decision making process because of the fact that they are dominated by the eldest member of the family. Another picture which emerges from the same analysis is that there are not very many cases where the younger members of the family come forward and take decision in the presence of elder member of the family because of the socio-cultural taboos. It is considered almost insulting to the elder member of the family if he is physically and mentally fit to take a leading role in the decision making process.

Age Composition of Urban Scheduled Caste Respondents

The urban scheduled caste respondents constitute about 27 per cent of the total scheduled caste respondents. The proportion of the urban scheduled caste respondents in the different age group varies and is not in conformity with the age composition of all scheduled caste respondents.

Table 4.4 : Age Composition of Urban Scheduled Caste Respondents

Age Group	*Age Range*	*No. of Respondents*	*%age to total*
Young Age	<30 years	42	14.05
Lower Middle Age	30-39 years	77	25.75
Upper Middle Age	40-49 years	83	27.76
Old Age	50 & above years	97	32.44
Total		**299**	**100.00**

Table 4.4 shows that 42 respondents constituting about 14 per cent of the total urban scheduled castes belong to the younger age group. This indicates that the younger generation of the urban population comes forward and takes leading role in the decision making process. The elder generation of the urban scheduled caste respondents account roughly 32 per cent of the total urban scheduled castes, which is less than aggregate picture of the rural scheduled castes in this category. The middle age respondents

altogether constitute about 54 per cent of the total urban scheduled caste respondents which is again a positive sign of the emerging role of the comparatively younger generation in the decision making process in case of family matters.

The above analysis of the age composition of the scheduled caste respondents clearly shows that there is an overall change in the role of the younger generation but still there is a lot more to be done to encourage this group of population to take active and leading role in the family affairs.

Age Composition of Non-Scheduled Caste Respondents

In order to make a comparative analysis of the transformation among the scheduled caste population, the non-scheduled caste respondents have also been considered and interviewed. They account about 26 per cent of the total respondents. A statement of the age composition of the non-scheduled caste respondents is represented in Table 4.5 which shows that the younger generation contributes about 14 per cent of the total non-scheduled caste respondents. The older generation contributes almost one-third of the total non-scheduled caste respondents which is in conformity with percentage of all respondents falling under this category. The younger middle age respondents account about 27 per cent of the total non-scheduled caste respondents, while the corresponding percentage of the upper middle age is about 26 per cent. As such the middle age non-scheduled caste respondents account roughly 52 per cent of the total non-scheduled caste respondents. Although the picture of the age composition of the non-scheduled caste respondents is encouraging but it needs to be further improved so

Table 4.5 : Age Composition of All Non-Scheduled Castes Respondents

Age Group	*Age Range*	*No. of Respondents*	*%age to total*
Young Age	<30 years	56	14.07
Lower Middle Age	30-39 years	106	26.63
Upper Middle Age	40-49 years	103	25.88
Old Age	50 & above years	133	33.42
Total		**398**	**100.00**

as the younger generation takes much more leading role in the decision making process.

Age Composition of Rural Non-Scheduled Caste Respondents

Table 4.5 gives the aggregate status of the age composition of the non-scheduled caste respondents but a closer look at the master table and the scrutiny of the questionnaire shows that there is a lot of difference in case of the position of rural and urban non-scheduled caste respondents. Therefore, an attempt has been made to group the rural and urban non-scheduled castes in different age categories and it is represented in Tables 4.6 and 4.7. It is evident from Table 4.6 that about 12 per cent of the

Table 4.6 : Age Composition of Rural Non-Scheduled Caste Respondents

Age Groups	*Age Ranges*	*No. of Respondents*	*%age to total*
Young Age	<30 years	42	12.69
Lower Middle Age	30-39 years	84	25.38
Upper Middle Age	40-49 years	93	28.09
Old Age	50 & above years	112	33.84
Total		**331**	**100.00**

total 331 rural non-scheduled caste respondents belong to the younger generation, which is almost identical to the rural scheduled caste respondents. But as we move upward in the age group the percentage of the rural non-scheduled castes does not match either with the rural scheduled caste respondents or even with the all rural scheduled caste respondents. Slightly more than one-third of the rural non-scheduled castes belong to the elder generation of 50 years and above which shows that even among the rural non-scheduled caste respondents their elder generation dominates the scene of decision making process regarding family affairs. It is also supported by the fact that the upper middle age represents 28 per cent of the rural non-scheduled caste respondents. The remaining one-fourth respondents belong to the lower middle age group. The analysis of the rural non-scheduled castes shows that in general they are in better position than the rural scheduled caste respondents. However, they also need to be convinced for handing over the responsibilities of the decision making process to younger generation which, perhaps, is more competent to take better decision in the light of their education and interaction of the people.

Age Composition of Urban Non-Scheduled Caste Respondents

A statistical account of the age composition of urban non-scheduled caste respondents is given in Table 4.7, which shows a different picture than the age composition of rural non-scheduled

Table 4.7 : Age Composition of Urban Non-Scheduled Caste Respondents

Age Group	*Age Range*	*No. of Respondents*	*%age to total*
Young Age	<30 years	14	20.89
Lower Middle Age	30-39 years	22	32.84
Upper Middle Age	40-49 years	10	14.93
Old Age	50 & above years	21	31.34
Total		**67**	**100.00**

caste respondents. The younger generation accounts more than one-fifth of the total 67 urban non-scheduled caste respondents. It may be inferred from this that the younger urban non-scheduled castes are more active and are taking leading role in the decision making process of family affairs. There are 21 respondents accounting roughly 31 per cent of the total urban non-scheduled caste respondents in the older age group, which is a lower percentage as compared to either total scheduled caste or non-scheduled caste respondents. Another interesting feature is that only 15 per cent of total non-urban scheduled castes fall under middle age group. It is also a testimony of the fact that the elder generation of non-scheduled caste respondents are gradually relinquishing their responsibility in the decision making process and passing it on to younger generation, which is more competent to take rational and reasonable decisions regarding the family affairs. The lower middle age accounts 33 per cent of the total respondents which is the highest percentage as compared to the other categories of the respondents falling in this age group.

Age Composition of All Rural Respondents

The analysis of the age composition of the respondents would be incomplete if we do not consider it with respect to the total rural and urban respondents because there is a dichotomy among these two categories of respondents. Therefore, a statistical account of these two categories is given in Tables 4.8 and 4.9 which show that a little more than three-fourth (75.8%) respondents are rural and the remaining (24.2%) fall in the urban category.

Table 4.8 : Age Composition of All Rural Respondents

Age Group	*Age Range*	*No. of Respondents*	*%age to total*
Young Age	<30 years	159	13.90
Lower Middle Age	30-39 years	301	26.31
Upper Middle Age	40-49 years	303	26.48
Old Age	50 & above years	381	33.31
Total		**1144**	**100.00**

Table 4.8 shows that almost exactly one-third rural respondents belong to the old age group of 50 years and above which is in conformity with the age composition of all respondents. The younger generation of this group of respondents account roughly 14 per cent whereas the respondents falling under lower middle age and upper middle age groups account almost an equal percentage to the entire rural respondents. It could be inferred from this analysis that the rural respondents need more counseling and constant encouragement to pass on the responsibilities to the younger generation which, according to the well established belief, is more competent to discharge the duties of the leadership in the family affairs.

Table 4.9 : Age Composition of All Urban Respondents

Age Group	*Age Range*	*No. of Respondents*	*%age to total*
Young Age	<30 years	56	15.30
Lower Middle Age	30-39 years	96	26.23
Upper Middle Age	40-49 years	92	25.14
Old Age	50& above years	122	33.33
Total		**366**	**100.00**

Age Composition of All Urban Respondents

The age composition of all urban respondents represents encouraging results. More than 15 per cent of all urban respondents belong to the younger generation but the older group of people account almost the same percentage as in case of all rural respondents. In case of the middle age group respondents, the lower middle age group contributes higher percentage (26.2%) as compared to the upper middle age group (25.1%). This is also a positive point as far as the decision making process in the family affairs is concerned.

It may be concluded that the younger generation is, by and large, coming forward in taking the leading role in the family matters but there are a lot of variations among various categories of respondents. For example, among the urban non-scheduled caste respondents the younger generation accounts 21 per cent, while among the rural scheduled caste respondents the corresponding figure is only 12.6 per cent.

Educational Status of Respondents

The role of education in the socio-economic transformation of the common masses in general and scheduled castes population in particular hardly needs any emphasis. It is considered to be one of the chief instruments through which a society socialises its members and brings desirable changes in its people. In fact education is the aggregate of all the process by means of which a person develops abilities, attitudes and other forms of behaviour of positive values in the society he lives in or it is a social process by which people are subjected to the influence of selected and controlled environment so that they can attain social competence and optimum individual development (Bear, 1947). As such it could be argued that education influences the course of behaviour of both society and its individuals. Various studies have proved that there is close relationship between educational level and socio-economic transformation (Ramaswamy, 1972, and Mohammad,1981).

As the educational attainment of the respondents varies from informal education with the simple ability of reading and writing in their mother-tongue without any formal certificate to Post-Graduate degree which are neither comparable nor can be aggregated. Hence, the following judicious scoring scheme has been evolved :

(i)	Illiterate	0.00
(ii)	Informal	0.25
(iii)	Primary	0.50
(iv)	Middle	0.75
(v)	High School	1.25
(vi)	Intermediate	1.75
(vii)	B.A.	2.50
(viii)	M.A. & other	3.50

Based on this scoring scheme, the total score of each respondent has been ascertained. Finally, they have been arranged in ascending order and divided into four categories (Table 4.10) which shows that 737 out of 1510 respondents accounting to nearly 49 per cent are illiterate which is a very discouraging

Table 4.10 : Educational Status of All Respondents

Category	*Score Range*	*No. of Respondents*	*%age to total*
Illiterate	0.0	737	48.81
Less Educated	Below 1.5	653	43.25
Moderately Educated	1.5-2.5	109	7.22
Highly Educated	2.6 & above	11	0.72
Total		**1510**	**100.00**

picture. It also shows that about 48 per cent of the respondents are literate which is far below the national and the state average. Another discouraging picture which emerges is that nearly 43 per cent of the respondents are less educated. Hence, it leaves only 8 per cent for moderately and highly educated respondents. Even out of this 8 per cent, the lion's share (7.2%) goes to the moderately educated and remaining 0.72 per cent goes to highly educated respondents. A closer look of the summary table and the scrutiny of the questionnaire reveals that the majority of the educated respondents belong to the younger age group, while much larger percentage of the elder group seems to be illiterate or very poorly educated (Fig.4.3). This further shows that the various programmes and policies of the government for the uplift of rural population specially in case of the scheduled caste population has started bearing the fruit but it has not affected the population on a large scale. However, there is a hope of improvement in the educational level of the rural people which is a sign of social transformation.

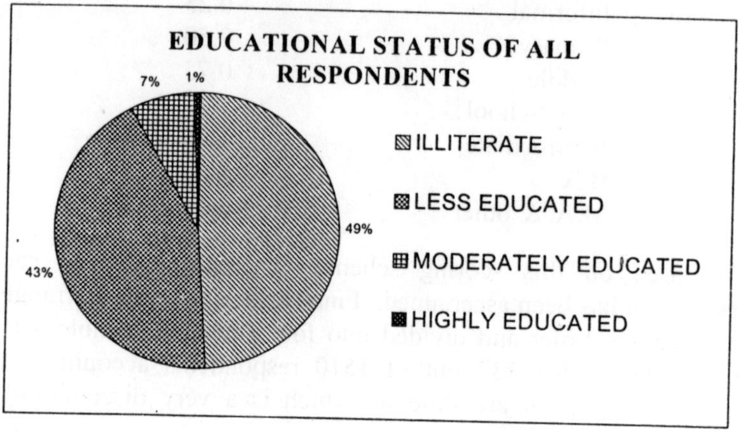

Fig. 4.3

Educational Status of All Scheduled Caste Respondents

As in case of age composition the educational status of the respondents also vary among the scheduled castes and non-scheduled castes as well as in case of urban and rural respondents. Therefore, in order to have a comprehensive view of literacy level among the respondents it has been examined at various levels. With this in view the educational status of the scheduled caste respondents has been presented in Table 4.11 which shows that about 56 per cent of the total 1112 respondents are illiterate, while

Table 4.11 : Educational Status of All Scheduled Caste Respondents

Category	*Score Range*	*No. of Respondents*	*%age to total*
Illiterate	0.0	627	56.38
Less educated	Below 1.5	427	38.40
Moderately size	1.5-2.5	54	4.86
Highly size	2.6 & above	4	0.36
Total		**1112**	**100.00**

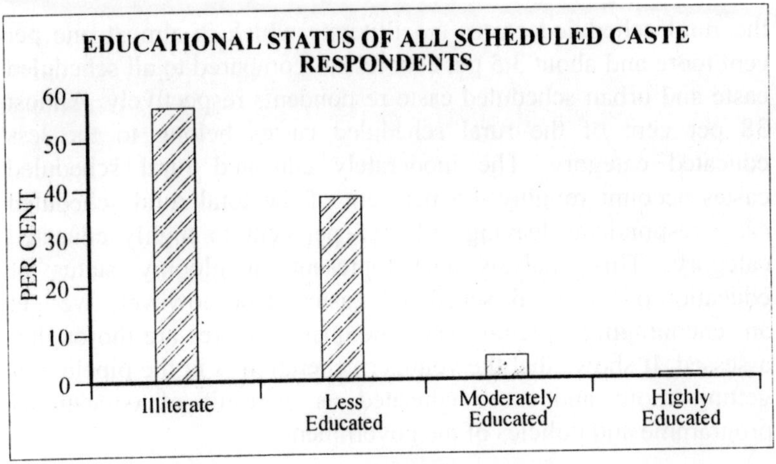

Fig. 4.4

about 38 per cent are less educated. As such these two categories together account roughly 95 per cent of the total scheduled caste respondents (Fig. 4.4). The remaining 5 per cent belong to moderately or highly educated categories. This analysis shows that the literacy status of scheduled caste is deplorably low and it needs to be improved. The only ray of hope we see when we look at the master table and scrutinise the questionnaires which show that the younger generation is inclined towards education and it is a sign of social transformation.

Educational Status of Rural Scheduled Caste Respondents

The analysis of Table 4.11 shows the aggregate picture of all scheduled caste respondents but there are rural-urban differential in it. Hence, an attempt has been made to analyse it in Tables 4.12 and 4.13. It emerges from Table 4.12 that more than 57 per cent of

Table 4.12 : Educational Status of Rural Scheduled Caste Respondents

Category	*Score Range*	*No. of Respondents*	*%age to total*
Illiterate	0.0	466	57.32
Less Educated	Below 1.5	307	37.76
Moderately Educated	1.5-2.5	36	4.43
Highly Educated	2.6 & above	4	0.49
Total		**813**	**100.00**

the rural scheduled castes are illiterate which is almost one per cent more and about 3.5 per cent less as compared to all scheduled caste and urban scheduled caste respondents respectively. Almost 38 per cent of the rural scheduled castes belong to the less educated category. The moderately educated rural scheduled castes account roughly 4.5 per cent of the total rural scheduled caste respondents leaving only 0.5 per cent to highly educated category. This analysis also represents a gloomy status of education of the rural scheduled castes. But, however, we get an encouraging picture when the questionnaires are thoroughly assessed. It shows that the younger generation is in the pipeline of getting more and more educated as a result of educational programme and policies of the government.

Educational Status of Urban Scheduled Caste Respondents

The educational status of the urban scheduled caste is comparatively more encouraging (Table 4.13). There are 18 out of 299 urban scheduled caste respondents who are moderately educated. But interestingly there is not even a single respondent falling in the highly educated category. Like the general pattern,

Table 4.13 : Educational Status of Urban Scheduled Caste Respondents

Category	*Score Range*	*No.of Respondents*	*%age to total*
Illiterate	0.0	161	53.85
Less Educated	Below 1.5	120	40.13
Moderately Educated	1.5-2.5	18	6.02
Highly Educated	2.6 & above	-	-
Total		**299**	**100.00**

the illiterate respondents contribute 54 per cent of the total respondents, whereas about 40 per cent is constituted by the less educated respondents. As such about 95 per cent of the total urban scheduled caste respondents are in a poor state of affairs as far as education is concerned. However, with the encouraging and constant efforts of the government through its educational policies and programmes, the younger generation is venturing in the field of education.

Educational Status of Non-Scheduled Caste Respondents

A comparative review of the educational status of scheduled caste and non-scheduled caste respondents indicates that the non-scheduled castes are on the whole in a better position than the scheduled caste respondents. Table 4.14 shows that 116 out of 398 respondents amounting to roughly 29 per cent of total non-scheduled caste respondents are illiterate which is much lower than the scheduled caste respondents. The less educated group of respondents accounts about 56 per cent of the total respondents. This is a very encouraging scene towards the popularity and utilization of educational facilities. It clearly shows that the younger generation is coming up in case of the education. In this case the percentage is much higher than the scheduled caste respondents.

Table 4.14 : Educational Status of All Non-Scheduled Caste Respondents

Category	*Score Range*	*No. of Respondents*	*%age to total*
Illiterate	0.0	116	29.15
Less Educated	Below 1.5	222	55.78
Moderately Educated	1.5-2.5	53	13.31
Highly Educated	2.6 & above	7	1.76
Total		**398**	**100.00**

Table 4.14 further shows that 53 respondents amounting to more than 13 per cent of total non-scheduled caste respondents are moderately educated. This is again 8 per cent higher than the corresponding category of scheduled castes. Seven respondents belong to the highly educated category with the educational score of more than 2.6. This analysis clearly indicates that the level of literacy is increasing and is likely to increase even faster in the near future which is a clear sign of social transformation.

Educational Status of Rural Non-Scheduled Caste Respondents

Table 4.14 gives an aggregate picture of the literacy level of the non-scheduled caste respondents but there are variations in it according to the rural and urban respondents. Hence, an attempt has been made to highlight this differential among them in Tables 4.15 and 4.16. Table 4.15 shows that the rural non-scheduled caste account roughly 83 per cent of the total non-scheduled caste respondents. Out of this about 29 per cent are illiterate, while 179 respondents amounting to about 54 per cent of rural non-scheduled caste respondents fall in the less educated category. There are about 15 per cent respondents under moderately educated category, while 6 respondents covering about 2 per cent of total rural non-scheduled castes are highly educated. The overall picture which emerges from facts and figure of this table is that the literacy level is heading towards positive direction and in the near future not only more people would be educated but literacy standard will also increase.

Table 4.15 : Educational Status of Rural Non-Scheduled Caste Respondents

Category	*Score Range*	*No. of Respondents*	*%age to total*
Illiterate	0.0	95	28.70
Less Educated	Below 1.5	179	54.07
Moderately Educated	1.5-2.5	51	15.41
Highly Educated	2.6 & above	6	1.82
Total		**331**	**100.00**

Educational Status of Urban Non-Scheduled Caste Respondents

The literacy level of the urban non-scheduled caste respondents is the highest among all different categories of respondents. Table 4.16 shows that out of 67 urban non-scheduled caste respondents, 21 respondents contributing about 31 per cent of the

Table 4.16 : Educational Status of Urban Non-Scheduled Caste Respondents

Category	*Score Range*	*No. of Respondents*	*%age to total*
Illiterate	0.0	21	31.35
Less Educated	Below 1.5	43	64.18
Moderately Educated	1.5-2.5	3	4.47
Highly Educated	2.6 & above	—	—
Total		**67**	**100.00**

total are illiterate, while about 64 per cent respondents fall under less educated category which is a clear indicator of the fact that the literacy level is picking up and is likely to increase more within a short period of time. There are only 3 respondents accounting about 4.5 per cent of the urban non-scheduled caste respondents who are moderately educated. Interestingly there is not even a single respondent in the highly educated category.

Educational Status of Rural Respondents

It would be worthwhile if an analysis of the literacy level of the respondents is done according to rural and urban respondents. Therefore, the former is shown in Table 4.17 while the later is represented in Table 4.18. It emerges from Table 4.17 that almost

Table 4.17 : Educational Status of Rural Respondents

Category	*Score Range*	*No. of Respondents*	*%age to total*
Illiterate	0.0	562	49.13
Less Educated	Below 1.5	484	42.32
Moderately Educated	1.5-2.5	88	7.69
Highly Educated	2.6 & above	10	0.86
Total		**1144**	**100.00**

half of the rural respondents are illiterate, while only 10 respondents accounting to less than one per cent of the total are in the highly educated category with an educational score of more than 2.5. This table further shows that about 42 per cent rural respondents belong to less educated category, while the moderately educated category covers 7.7 per cent of the rural respondents. It may be inferred from this table that the status of education of the rural population is not in a good state of affairs but there is a ray of hope for increasing the literacy level among the younger generation.

Educational Status of Urban Respondents

The picture of the literacy level of the urban respondents is satisfactory and encouraging. Table 4.18 shows that about 48 per cent of the total urban respondents are illiterate, while around 46 per cent are less educated. The moderately educated category covers around 5.7 per cent of the urban respondents while there is only one respondent covering just 0.27 per cent falls under highly educated category. This analysis indicates that the status of urban literacy is not very encouraging and satisfactory. Therefore, a lot needs to be done in order to improve literacy level among the respondents.

Table 4.18 : Educational Status of Urban Respondents

Category	*Score Range*	*No. of Respondents*	*%age to total*
Illiterate	0.0	175	47.82
Less Educated	Below 1.5	169	46.17
Moderately Educated	1.5-2.5	21	5.74
Highly Educated	2.6 & above	1	0.27
Total		**366**	**100.00**

Educational Status of the Households

In the preceding pages the role and significance of education in the process of socio-economic transformation has already been discussed. The evaluation of educational status of respondents has shown a lot of variations at different levels among the selected respondents. It is believed that it is not only the educational status of the respondents but the overall educational index of the household which matters a lot in socio-economic transformation. With this view an attempt has been made to calculate the educational index of the household. Following the same scoring scheme used in the assessment of educational status of respondents the scores have been given to all the individual members of the family as per their educational standards. The educational score of the family members have been added together and have been divided by the total family member except those falling in the age group of less than 5 years. It is observed from Table 4.19 that almost half of the households belong to illiterate

Table 4.19 : Educational Status of All Households

Category	*Score Range*	*No. of Households*	*%age to total*
Illiterate	0.0	737	48.81
Less Educated	Below 1.5	653	43.25
Moderately Educated	1.5-2.5	109	7.22
Highly Educated	2.6 & above	11	0.72
Total		**1510**	**100.00**

category with zero score, while about 43 per cent fall under the low educated category with less than 1.5 score. As such about 92 per cent households are poorly educated (Fig. 4.5). It represents a very sad state of affairs regarding the educational level. But when we scrutinize the questionnaire and have a closer look at the master table we get some rays of hope. The younger generation seems to be coming up while the older generations are illiterate and have very poor education. That is why the educational index of the substantial number of households has gone down. However, looking at the trend of education among the younger generation there is a hope that the educational index would go up in near future. Table 4.21 further reveals that less than one per cent belong to the high category of educational index, while a little more than 7 per cent have moderate educational status.

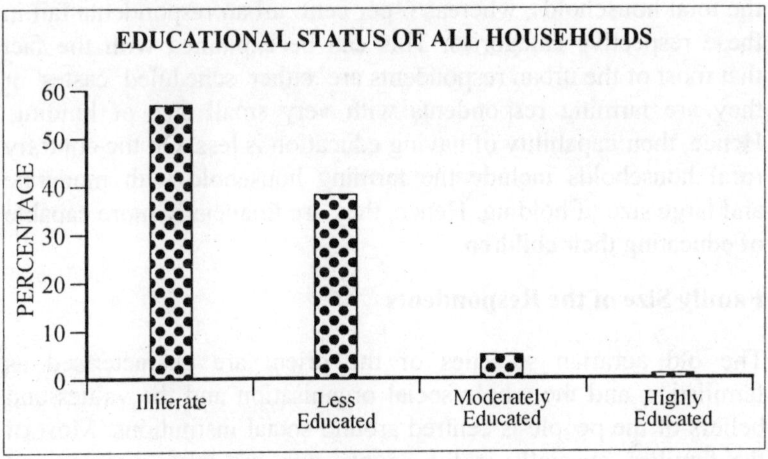

Fig. 4.5

The aggregate picture of educational index of the household is almost reflected in the educational index of the household of rural-urban respondents in Tables 4.20 and 4.21. However, the

Table 4.20 : Educational Status of Rural Households

Category	*Score Range*	*No. of Households*	*%age to total*
Illiterate	0.0	562	49.13
Less educated	Below 1.5	484	42.31
Moderately educated	1.5-2.5	88	7.70
Highly educated	2.6 & above	10	0.86
Total		**1144**	**100.00**

Table 4.21 : Educational Status of Urban Households

Category	*Score Range*	*No. of Households*	*%age to total*
Illiterate	0.0	175	47.82
Low educated	Below 1.5	169	46.17
Moderately educated	1.5-2.5	21	5.74
Highly educated	2.6 & above	1	0.27
Total		**366**	**100.00**

interesting point is that the urban households are less educated than their rural counterpart respondents. The moderately and highly educated rural respondents account around 8 per cent of the total households, whereas 6 per cent urban respondents fall in these respective categories. This can be explained with the fact that most of the urban respondents are either scheduled castes or they are farming respondents with very small size of holding. Hence, their capability of having education is less. On the contrary rural households include the farming household with moderate and large size of holding. Hence, they are financially more capable of educating their children.

Family Size of the Respondents

The old agrarian societies of the orient are characterised as familistics, and the whole social organisation and the values and beliefs of the people is centred around social institutions. Most of the families, specially in the countryside, are large in sizes and extended or joint in composition. Parents generally live with their married sons and their families. By and large, it is the family, instead of the individuals, which is the unit of social action. The thought and actions of the individual members in the family, in a large measure, are influenced by the family as a single entity. The personality of a member of a large family is somewhat different from that of a member belonging to a small family. Hence, the size of a family has a major role in deciding the type of occupation to be adopted as well as in the process of its development. Therefore, the total member of the selected respondents were enumerated during the course of the fieldwork. In the present study the family includes all the members of selected respondents who live in one household and share the single kitchen. On the basis of the total members of the household, families were arranged in ascending order, and finally, grouped into five categories (Table 4.22).

Table 4.22 : Family Size of All Respondents

Category	*Size of the family*	*No. of Households*	*%age to total*
Small size	<5 members	335	22.18
Medium size	5-9 members	869	57.55
Large size	10-14 members	232	15.37
Very large size	15-19 members	65	4.31
Extremely large size	20 & above	9	0.59
Total		**1510**	**100.00**

As is evident from Table 4.22 that the size of family ranges from 2 members to more than 20 members. The small size of family accounts roughly 22 per cent of the total households, while the medium size covers roughly 58 per cent of the total households. As such almost 80 per cent of the respondents belong to small and medium size of family which shows a positive sign of social transformation (Fig.4.6).

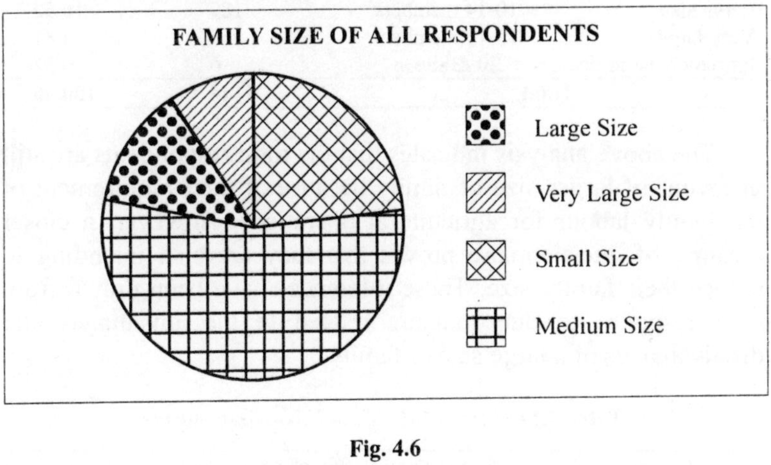

Fig. 4.6

The respondents are realizing the importance and advantages of smaller size of family as compared to large ones. The large size of family accounts roughly 15 per cent of the total number of households, while the very large and extremely large size put together cover only 5 per cent of the total households. This is again the testimony of the fact that the people do not prefer large size of family.

The above analysis presents an aggregate picture of the family size but there are a lot of variations in size of family among the rural and urban households. A comparative structure of the family size of both rural and urban is presented in Tables 4.23 and 4.24. Table 4.23 shows a slightly different picture of the composition of the family as compared to the total respondents. About 22 per cent of the households belong to the small size of family with less than 5 members, while around 57 per cent fall in the category of medium size of family. Both together account about 78 per cent of the total households. The large size of families together account around 22 per cent of the total households. Out of which about 60 per cent belong to large size while the remaining 5 per cent fall in the category of very large and extremely large size of family.

Table 4.23 : Family Size of All Rural Respondents

Category	*Member of the family*	*No. of Resp.*	*%age to total*
Small size	<5 members	243	21.24
Medium size	5-9 members	651	56.91
Large size	10-14 members	189	16.52
Very large size	15-19 members	55	4.81
Extremely large size	20 & above	6	0.52
Total		**1144**	**100.00**

The above analysis indicates that the rural respondents are still in favour of larger size of family because of their requirement of the family labour for agricultural operations. However, a closer scrutiny of questionnaire proves that they are also intending to reduce their family size. These inferences have been drawn from their response to questionnaire related to the advantages and disadvantages of a large size of family.

Table 4.24 : Family Size of All Urban Respondents

Category	*Size of the family*	*No. of Respondents*	*%age to total*
Small size	<5 members	92	25.14
Medium size	5-9 size	218	59.56
Large size	10-14 size	43	11.75
Very large size	15-19 size	10	2.73
Extremely large size	20 & above	3	0.82
Total		**366**	**100.00**

The size of the family of the urban respondents represented in Table 4.24 gives more encouraging results. Among the urban respondents more than one-fourth of the total have a small size of family, while nearly 60 per cent belong to the medium size of family. As such about 85 per cent of the urban households have their families belonging to a family size with less than 9 members. The large size of the family accounts a little more than one-tenth of the households, while only 3 respondents are covered in extremely large size of family. This comparative size of family of rural-urban highlights that urban respondents are more alert and aware of the advantages of small size of family. Hence, majority of them have the smaller size of family. Therefore, it is suggested that the idea of small size of family should be encouraged and propagated.

Economic Structure of Respondents

Like social structure, economic structure of the respondents also plays a significant role in the process of transformation of the people of all castes in general and the scheduled castes in particular. It has been observed that the process of economic transformation is comparatively more quick and rapid among the people with better economic status than the people with lower ones. Therefore, the economic structure of respondents including size of holding, patterns of landuse in both kharif and rabi seasons, level of innovativeness have been discussed here. The other economic parameters have been described and explained in the chapter dealing with economic transformation.

Size of Landholding of Respondents

There is intrinsic relationship between size of holding and socio-economic transformation. The sociological and anthropological studies provide enough evidence to prove the fact that the extent of land ownership is an important indicator of one's socio-economic status. It is more so in an essentially agricultural country like India where land, being scarce, is much valued by the people. There are mainly two types of landholdings, viz. actual and operational. Actual size of holding includes all the land entered in the name of an individual in the government records irrespective of the fact whether he cultivates it by himself or not, whereas operational size of holding is the land on which the farmers operate to produce agricultural commodities. In the present study only operational size of holdings have been taken into consideration because majority of the respondents being scheduled caste do not own the land. Only some of the non-scheduled caste respondents own the land.

In our country in general and in the state of Uttar Pradesh in particular, there is complex tennurial system, although the state and the central governments are trying to simplify it by enacting various legislation from time to time. But unfortunately or fortunately, the Indians are masterminded in finding the loopholes in the law or interpreting the laws in their own favour against its spirit. And as such, practically the tennurial system becomes more and more complex, although theoretically it is being simplified and reformed. However, the owners of land, who are not in a position to cultivate their land themselves, or who do not want to cultivate their land themselves, give their land to actual tiller on various terms and conditions. The nature of the term and conditions depends on the supply and demand of land to be leased out. If the demand is more and supply is meagre, the owner of land exploits the tiller by giving his land to him (*tiller*) according to his term and conditions. For example, in eastern and central Uttar Pradesh, the tiller has to bear the entire cost of inputs, except the land rent which the owner has to pay, but the entire agricultural products are shared by both on equal basis. On the contrary, when supply of land is more and demand is less, the tillers of land dictate the terms, and the owner has to accept it. For example, in western Uttar Pradesh the owner of the land, besides paying the land rent to government, has also to pay 50 per cent input cost, otherwise he would be given only 40 per cent share or even less than it.

Nevertheless, whatever may be the tenancy system, it is the total area being cultivated by the respondents which matters more than the land registered in his name because it is only this size of holding in which he has to toil and supply all his inputs. Therefore, in the present study an attempt has been made to find out the operational size of holding of each respondent. After working out the operational size of holding of each respondent, they have been arranged in ascending order and finally, classified into five categories (Table 4.25).

It is evident from Table 4.25 that only 34 per cent of the total respondents practice agriculture with different size of holdings. The remaining 994 respondents covering 66 per cent of the respondents are landless because majority of them are scheduled

Table 4.25 : Operational Size of Holding of All Respondents

Category	*Acreage Range*	*No. of Respondents*	*%age to total*
Land less	–	994	65.83
Marginal Size	<2.50	373	24.70
Small size	2.50-5.00	93	6.16
Semi Medium size	5.01-10.00	35	2.32
Medium size	>10.00	15	0.99
Total		**1510**	**100.00**

castes who neither own the land nor have enough money and infrastructure facilities to engage themselves in agricultural activities. Among the farmers practicing agriculture about 72 per cent are operating on marginal size of holding which is also very uneconomical (Fig. 4.7). Nearly one-tenth of the farming respondents operate in medium size of holding, while 93 respondents amounting to about 18 per cent of the farming respondents operate on small size of holding ranging from 2.5 to 5 acres. The above discussion clearly indicates that the size of holding is extremely small among the farming respondents.

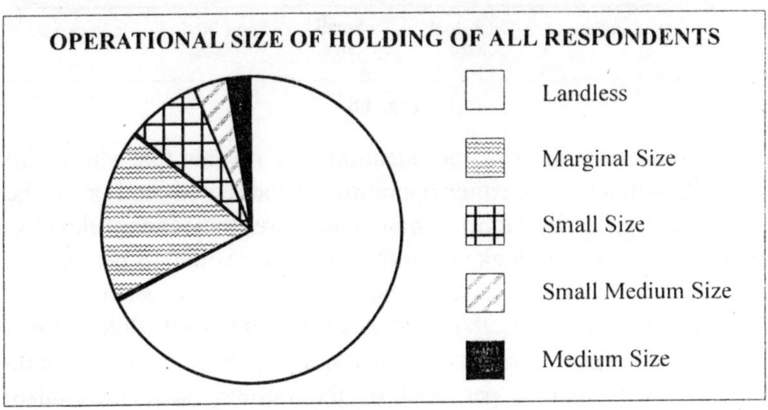

Fig. 4.7

Size of Holding of All Scheduled Castes

The above analysis shows the aggregate picture of operational size of holding but there are differences in it among the different types of respondents. Therefore, Table 4.26 shows the operational size of holding of scheduled caste respondents. It indicates that around 72 per cent of the scheduled caste respondents are landless, while around 24 per cent operate on marginal size of holding (Fig. 4.8).

Table 4.26 : Operational Size of Holding of All Scheduled Caste Respondents

Category	*Acreage Range*	*No. of Respondents*	*%age to total*
Landless	—	802	72.12
Marginal Size	<2.50	261	23.48
Small size	2.50-5.00	41	3.68
Semi Medium size	5.01-10.00	7	0.63
Medium size	>10.00	1	0.09
Total		**1112**	**100.00**

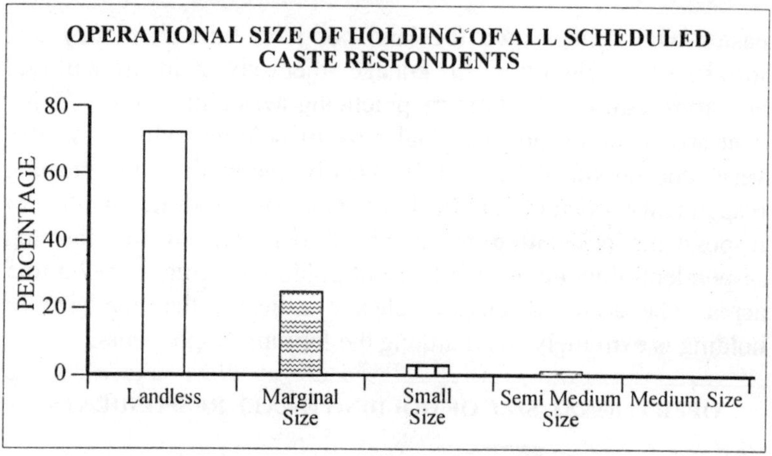

Fig. 4.8

A closer scrutiny of the questionnaire reveals that almost all these respondents are either operating on the rented land or on the *Patta* land given by Gram Samaj. Therefore, they cannot develop their agriculture and make it more profitable. About 13 per cent of the farming scheduled caste respondents operate on small size of holding. As such about 98 per cent of the farming scheduled castes operate on very small size of holding. Only 8 respondents covering less than 2 per cent of the farming scheduled caste respondents operate on semi-medium size of holding. Among the scheduled caste respondents there is a difference in the operational size of holding among rural and urban respondents.

Size of Holding of Rural Scheduled Castes

Table 4.27 showing the operational size of holding of rural scheduled castes indicates that about two-thirds of the respondents of this category are landless, while about 30 per cent operate on marginal size of holding. On top of it 4 per cent respondents have reported to be operating on small size of holding. As such almost 100 per cent farming rural scheduled caste respondents except one are either landless or operate on the small size of holding.

Table 4.27 : Operational Size of Holding of Rural Scheduled Caste Respondents

Category	Acreage Range	No. of Respondents	%age to total
Landless	—	533	65.56
Marginal Size	<2.50	246	30.26
Small size	2.50-5.00	33	4.06
Semi Medium size	5.01-10.00	1	0.12
Medium size	>10.00	—	—
Total		**813**	**100.00**

Size of Holding of Urban Scheduled Castes

The position of urban scheduled caste respondents in this respect is slightly encouraging. About 90 per cent of urban respondents are landless and only 10 per cent operate on different size of holdings (Table 4.28). Out of this 5 per cent and nearly 3 per cent operate on marginal and small size of holding, whereas only 2 per cent respondents operate on semi-medium size of holding. This is because of the fact that the urban owners of the land, by and

Table 4.28 : Operational Size of Holding of Urban Scheduled Caste Respondents

Category	*Acreage Range*	*No. of Respondents*	*%age to total*
Landless	—	269	89.97
Marginal size	<2.50	15	5.02
Small size	2.50-5.00	8	2.67
Semi-Medium size	5.01-10.00	6	2.01
Medium size	>10.00	1	0.33
Total		**299**	**100.00**

large, rent out their land to these scheduled caste respondents because their size of holding is too small to be operated by themselves on commercial basis. Therefore, they make themselves free to be engaged in other activities by renting out their land. These poor farmers utilise their land mainly for vegetable farming.

Size of Holding of All Non-Scheduled Caste Respondents

The status of operational size of holding of non-scheduled caste respondents is comparatively better. About 48 per cent respondents under this category are landless, while 52 per cent operate on differential size of land holding (Table 4.29). Around

Table 4.29 : Operational Size of Holding of All Non-scheduled Caste Respondents

Category	*Acreage Range*	*No. of Respondents*	*%age to total*
Landless	—	192	48.24
Marginal size	<2.50	112	28.14
Small size	2.50-5.00	52	13.06
Semi Medium size	5.01-10.00	28	7.04
Medium size	>10.00	14	3.52
Total		**398**	**100.00**

54 per cent of the farming respondents of this category operate on marginal size of holding, while a little more than one-fourth toil on small size of holding. As such around 80 per cent of the respondents of this category work on smaller size of holding. Nearly 20 per cent operate on medium size of holding of which around 14 per cent work on the semi-medium size of holding.

Size of Holding of Rural Non-Scheduled Caste Respondents

Among the non-scheduled caste respondents also there is a difference between the rural and urban respondents. Table 4.30 indicates that about 43 per cent of the rural non-scheduled caste respondents are landless, while 57 per cent are operating on different size of holding. Among the farming respondents of this category about 55 per cent have marginal size of holding, while 26 per cent operate on small size of holding. As such 81 per cent respondents operate on smaller size of holding . The respondents operating on medium size of holding account less than 20 per cent of the respondents under this category. Out of this about two-thirds work on semi-medium, while the remaining one-third

Table 4.30 : Operational Size of Holding of Rural Non-Scheduled Caste Respondents

Category	*Acreage Range*	*No. of Respondents*	*%age to total*
Landless	—	142	42.90
Marginal size	<2.50	103	31.12
Small size	2.50-5.00	50	15.10
Semi Medium size	5.01-10.00	24	7.25
Medium size	>10.00	12	3.63
Total		**331**	**100.00**

operate on medium size of holding. Here again the closure scrutiny of the questionnaire clearly reveals that even the majority of the non-scheduled caste respondents operate on rental land holdings. A very small number of them have their own agricultural land.

Size of Holding of Urban Non-Scheduled Caste Respondents

There are only 67 non-scheduled caste urban respondents accounting to about 17 per cent of the respondents under this category. Table 4.31 indicates that a little less than three-fourths of the urban non-scheduled caste respondents are landless, which stands to reasons. Out of the remaining one-fourth about 30 per cent operate on marginal size of holding, while 3 per cent toil on

Table 4.31 : Operational Size of Holding of Urban Non-Scheduled Caste Respondents

Category	*Acreage Range*	*No. of Respondents*	*% age to total*
Landless	—	50	74.63
Marginal size	<2.50	9	13.44
Small size	2.50-5.00	2	2.98
Semi-Medium size	5.01-10.00	4	5.97
Medium size	>10.00	2	2.98
Total		**67**	**100.00**

small size of holdings. The medium size of holding covers about 9 per cent of the respondents. Out of which 6 per cent belong to the semi-medium category and the remaining 3 per cent belong to medium size of holding. The above picture in this case is due to the non-availability of agricultural land in the urban areas. In fact it is either the urban fringe or the vacant land within the urban centre which is utilised for agricultural operations.

Size of Holding of All Rural and Urban Respondents

Interesting results emerge when we compare the operational size of holding of all rural and urban respondents. It is evident from Tables 4.32 and 4.33 that about 59 per cent rural respondents are landless, while 87 per cent urban respondents fall under this category. Nearly 31 per cent of the rural respondents have marginal size of holding (Table 4.32), whereas only 6 per cent of the urban respondents fall under this category (Table 4.33).

Table 4.32 : Operational Size of Holding of All Rural Respondents

Category	*Acreage Range*	*No. of Respondents*	*%age to total*
Landless	—	675	59.01
Marginal size	<2.50	349	30.51
Small size	2.50-5.00	83	7.25
Semi-Medium size	5.01-10.00	25	2.18
Medium size	10.00	12	1.05
Total		**1144**	**100.00**

Table 4.33 : Operational Size of Holding of All Urban Respondents

Category	*Acreage Range*	*No. of Respondents*	*% age to total*
Landless	-	319	87.16
Marginal size	<2.50	24	6.56
Small size	2.50-5.00	10	2.73
Semi-Medium size	5.01-10.00	10	2.73
Medium size	10.00	3	0 81
Total		**366**	**100.00**

Likewise around 7 per cent of the rural respondents operate on small size of holding, while about 3 per cent of urban respondent fall under this category. In case of medium size of holding, the situation in both the cases is almost similar. This large differential in operational size of holding of rural and urban can easily be explained in terms of availability of land, which is much more in the rural areas as compared to urban centres.

Pattern of Land Use

By and large, all the farming respondents devote their land to cultivation of crops during the two agricultural reasons: Kharif and Rabi. A very insignificant per cent of their land is devoted to orchards and groves. The percentage of such land is higher among the farmers of large size of holding. There are two basic reasons for this: the farmers of large size of holding are unable to manage their entire holdings. Hence, they devote some percentage of it to orchards and groves; secondly, due to rising cost of agricultural inputs specially the labour cost, the large size of farmers find it more profitable to plant orchards of mango, guava, jackal fruits etc. as compared to crop farming. During sixties and seventies, due to introduction of new technology in agriculture specially in case of irrigation, chemical fertilizers, improved varieties of seed and agricultural implements, the area under fallow, specially under current fallow, has considerably decreased, and the area under double and multiple cropping has gone up substantially. As a result the agricultural production has also increased. But now the agricultural pattern is taking new shape. The prices of agricultural inputs have gone up and there is shortage of labour in agriculture. Moreover, the agricultural labourers have started working according to fixed time schedule and duty, which do not suit agricultural operations. Consequently the total cost of agricultural inputs has gone up. On the contrary, the prices of agricultural products are low. Therefore, all those farmers who require the help of labourers, either due to large size of holding or due to small size of family, find agriculture as non-profitable business. Therefore, they are diverting their attention towards the plantation of various varieties of mango, guava, jackal fruit and eucalyptus trees. Among these, the lion's share goes to eucalyptus plantation which is also being propagated by government under afforestation scheme and social forestry programmes. However, this phenomenon is in initial stage and it has started in western, central and eastern Uttar Pradesh in varying degrees. In the opinion of the author this practice should be discouraged and the government should seriously think over it. Either the prices of agricultural products should be increased or the prices of agricultural inputs should be reduced so that agriculture becomes a profitable occupation. However, it would be worthwhile to discuss in brief the salient features of cropping patterns adopted by the respondents during kharif and rabi seasons.

Pattern of Landuse in Kharif Season

Kharif is the first season of agricultural year in India and the state too. It occupies about 43 per cent of the total cropped area cultivated by respondents in the selected villages. Out of which about 60 per cent is irrigated and the rest is unirrigated. Cereals are the major crops of this season occupying about 70 per cent of net cropped land in Kharif season. Rice, which is grown by almost every farmer in some quantity or the other, occupies a place of pride among kharif crops by occupying about 39 per cent of kharif cropped land. Prior to introduction of new varieties of seed and new agricultural technology, rice was a rainfed crop, but after sixties substantial percentage of it is also irrigated. Table 4.33 gives a statistical account of the areal strength together with the percentages under each of the major kharif crops. It is obvious from Table 4.33 that the entire agricultural land is devoted to the cultivation of kharif season. Rice occupying about 763 acres amounting to about 73 per cent of the total agricultural land (Table 4.33), is the predominant crop among the respondents which is in conformity with agricultural landscape of the state (Fig.4.9).

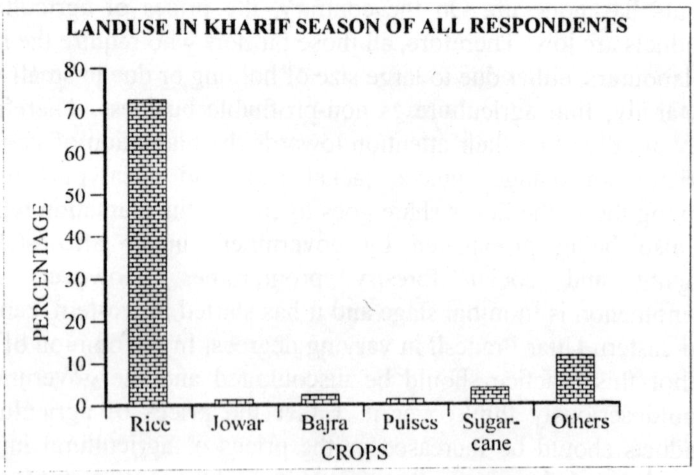

Fig. 4.9

The overall geographical conditions specially relief, climate and soil are very conducive for the cultivation of this crops. The modern agricultural infrastructure specially improvement in irrigation facilities have made it more popular even in the western part of the state. Sugarcane which is the commercial crop of the state is next important crop of this season. It occupies nearly 62 acres of land covering about 6 per cent of the total cropped area (Table 4.34). A close scrutiny of the master table and the questionnaire clearly indicates that the cultivation of sugarcane is more concentrated in two pockets of the state, viz. northeastern part and western part. In the former the basic cause of higher concentration is the fertile *bhat* soil which is rich in calcium, and has high water table facilitating easy and cheap irrigation, while in the latter the cheap canal irrigation water coupled with high level of agricultural technology are the main causes. However, it is a main source of income for the farmers of both the regions. Bajra is another crop of some significance occupying roughly 3.6 per cent of the total cropped area. It is mostly cultivated by the respondents of the western Uttar Pradesh. It is cultivated as a cereal as well as a fodder crop. It survives on less fertile soil with lower amount of moisture. Jowar is another course grain crop occupying a little more than one per cent of the area cultivated by the respondents. Jowar and Bajra are, by and large, grown in the same region and are used by poor farmers. Pulses — the main source of protein for the farmers is not a popular crop among the respondents. It occupies just a little more than one per cent of the total kharif cropped land. In spite of its being a remunerative crop, it does not have large area under it mainly because it is a crop which is more susceptible to weather condition. There is a lot of uncertainty in cultivation of pulses.

Table 4.34 : Land use in Kharif Season of All Respondents

Crops	*Area (in acres)*	*%age to total*
Rice	763.21	73.08
Jowar	13.35	1.28
Bajra	37.62	3.60
Pulses	14.01	1.34
Sugarcane	61.98	5.94
Others	154.18	14.76
Total	**1044.35**	**100.00**

Besides these, there are many other crops which are grown by the respondents. They are too numerous to be accounted separately. Moreover, the area under each of these crops is not large enough to be given under its heading. Hence, they have been put together and they account about 9 per cent of the kharif cropped area. It includes crops like maize, small millets, oilseeds, fibre crops, etc. Most of these crops are grown on subsistence basis.

All the vegetables put together occupy about 60 acres of land covering about 6 per cent of the kharif cropped land. There are variety of vegetables which are cultivated on subsistence basis in the region. The respondents generally grow cabbage, raddish, tori, ladies finger etc. on a small piece of fertile land which is generally irrigated. The nature of crop varies from region to region.

The above analysis gives aggregate pictures of landuse pattern in kharif season among all the selected respondents but there are differences in it as is evident from Tables 4.35 and 4.36 indicating the landuse among rural and urban respondents. The basic difference between the two is that the rural respondents cultivate pulses, while the urban respondents have devoted a microscopic area under it and it is not worth including in the table; *secondly*,

Table 4.35 : Landuse in Kharif Season for Rural Respondents

Crops	*Area (in acres)*	*%age to total*
Rice	619.15	72.60
Jowar	12.10	1.42
Bajra	28.62	3.35
Pulses	14.01	1.65
Sugarcane	55.98	6.56
Others	122.93	14.42
Total	**852.79**	**100.00**

Table 4.36 : Landuse in Kharif Season for Urban Respondents

Crops	*Area (in acres)*	*%age to total*
Rice	144.06	75.21
Jowar	1.25	0.65
Bajra	9.00	4.69
Pulses	-	-
Sugarcane	6.00	3.13
Others	31.25	16.32
Total	**191.56**	**100.00**

urban respondents give more emphasis to the cultivation of various kind of vegetables. They grow it on commercial basis and it is more remunerative. It altogether occupies roughly 19 acres accounting to about 10 per cent of kharif cropped land, while the rural respondents devote only 8 acres covering about 4 per cent of the total kharif cropped land. The urban respondents give more emphasis on vegetable cultivation because there is a demand for it in urban centres. However, it is quite clear from these three tables that cereals occupy prime place in the utilization of agricultural land during kharif season.

Pattern of Land use in Rabi Season

Rabi is another important agricultural season in the state occupying about 45 per cent of the total cropped area (Fig.4.10). Almost all the area under wheat is not only irrigated but two or three waterings are given to the crop. Wheat is a very common crop across the state and is grown almost all over it. But a closer scrutiny of the master table and the questionnaire indicates that the concentration of wheat cultivation is comparatively more in western Uttar Pradesh than the rest of the state. This is mainly due to better agricultural infrastructural facilities and the enterprising nature of the respondents. It has also been observed that the respondents with larger size of holding devote more area to wheat cultivation than others.

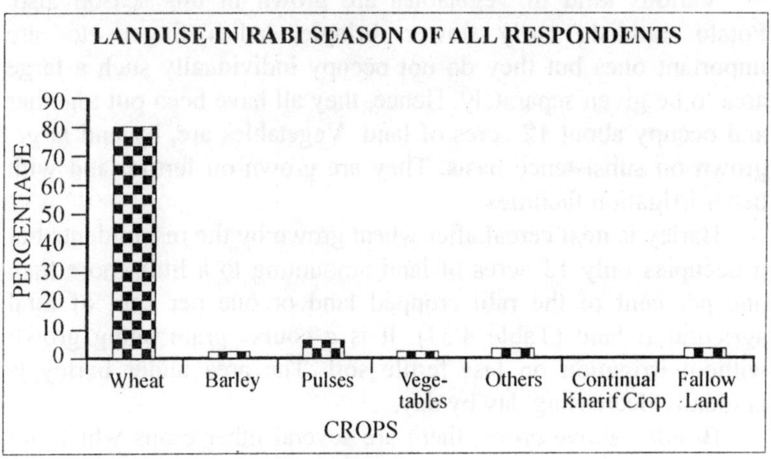

Fig.4.10

Pulses are the next important rabi crops covering nearly 54 acres of land which accounts 5.7 per cent of rabi cropped land or 5 per cent of the net agricultural land (Table 4.37). It includes variety of pulses but major ones are peas, gram and lentil which do not occupy such a large area to be accounted separately. Besides these, urad, moong, etc are other pulses grown in the state. Although pulses are in great demand and the prices are also high but their areal strength is not much because they are very vulnerable to weather condition. Hailstorm, frost and cloudy weather are very injurious to these crops. Besides, they are very susceptible to various kinds of insects and pests which damage the crop within no time. Hence, the poor respondents do not want to take risk in cultivating these crops.

Table 4.37 : Landuse in Rabi Season for All Respondents

Crops	*Area (in acres)*	*%age to total*	*%age to NSA*
Wheat	845.25	89.66	80.94
Barley	12.80	1.36	1.23
Pulses	53.57	5.68	5.13
Vegetables	11.74	1.25	1.12
Others	19.30	2.05	1.85
Continual Kharif crop	75.99	–	7.27
Fallow Land	25.70	–	2.46
Total	**1044.35**	**100.00**	**100.00**

Various kind of vegetables are grown in this season also. Potato, raddish, curly flower, bringle, ladies finger etc. are important ones but they do not occupy individually such a large area to be given separately. Hence, they all have been put together and occupy about 12 acres of land. Vegetables are, by and large, grown on subsistence basis. They are grown on fertile land with better irrigation facilities.

Barley is next cereal after wheat grown by the respondents but it occupies only 13 acres of land amounting to a little more than one per cent of the rabi cropped land or one per cent of total agricultural land (Table 4.37). It is a course grain being grown without irrigation on less fertile soil. The area under barley is gradually decreasing day by day.

Besides above crops, there are several other crops which are grown by the respondents. They are too numerous to be accounted individually. Hence, they have been put together under other crops and occupy about 19 acres of land which accounts roughly 2.0 per cent of rabi cropped land. The main crops included into it are lentil, tur, jai, etc.

Table 4.37 also shows that about 76 acres are covered by continual kharif crops (sugarcane and pulses) and nearly 26.0 acres are left fallow because of the deterioration of fertility of the soil. However, it may be concluded that during this season also cereals dominate the agricultural landscape.

A comparative statement of land use during rabi season by rural and urban respondents is given in Tables 4.38 and 4.39 which show certain difference among them. Firstly, rural respondents

Table 4.38 : Landuse in Rabi Season for Rural Respondents

Crops	*Area (in acres)*	*%age to total*	*%age to NSA*
Wheat	671.40	88.55	81.06
Barley	8.25	1.08	0.99
Pulses	49.85	6.57	6.02
Vegetables	9.49	1.25	1.15
Others	19.35	2.55	2.34
Continental Kharif crops	49.50	—	5.98
Fallow Land	20.42	—	2.46
Total	**828.26**	**100.00**	**100.00**

Table 4.39 : Landuse in Rabi Season for Urban Respondents

Crops	*Area (in acres)*	*%age to total*	*%age to NSA*
Wheat	173.85	94.32	80.45
Barley	4.50	2.44	2.08
Pulses	3.72	2.02	1.72
Vegetables	2.25	1.22	1.04
Continual Kharif crops	26.49	-	12.26
Fallow Land	5.28	-	2.45
Total	**216.09**	**100.00**	**100.00**

devote about 89 per cent to the cultivation of wheat, while urban respondents devote 94 per cent to it; and secondly, rural respondents devote about 7 per cent to pulse cultivation while their counterpart gives only 2 per cent.

Level of Innovativeness

The operational size of holdings and their mode of utilization during Kharif and Rabi seasons ascertain the economic status of the rural masses in India. Larger the size of holding coupled with high intensity of cropping together with high yield indicate the high economic status and *vice versa* is true in the opposite case. But the high intensity of cropping and high yield of crops are dependent on adoption of agricultural innovations such as farm implements, chemical fertilizers, high yielding varieties of seed, insecticides and pesticides and irrigation facilities. Therefore, data were collected regarding the adoption of these innovations during the fieldwork. As these innovations are of varied nature and character, they can not be added or averaged in order to calculate the composite index of adoption for the assessment of level of innovativeness. Hence, in order to bring all the innovations and the several variations in their adoption at uniform level, a well thought of scoring scheme has been used. The scores of individual respondents are added together in order to get his final scores. The respondents are arranged in ascending order on the basis of their score. Finally they have been grouped into 5 categories.

Level of Innovativeness of All Respondents

It is obvious from Table 4.40 that majority of the respondents are not very innovative. Roughly one-tenth of the total farming respondents are least innovative, while about 56 per cent are less innovative. As such about 67 per cent of the total farming respondents fall under this category (Fig.4.11). This is because of the fact that the scheduled caste farming respondents as well as the poor non-scheduled caste farming respondents fall under this category. They have neither the infrastructure nor the capital to adopt agricultural innovations. Roughly 15 per cent of the total farming respondents belong to highly and very highly category of level of innovativeness. A close look of the master table and the questionnaire indicates that they are the respondents with large size of holding and improved infrastructural facilities.

Table 4.40 : Level of Innovativeness of All Respondents

Category	*Score Range*	*No. of Respondents*	*%age to total*
Least Innovative	<1.50	50	11.44
Less Innovative	1.50-2.50	245	56.06
Moderately Innovative	2.51-5.00	76	17.40
Highly Innovative	5.01-7.50	41	9.38
Very Highly Innovative	>7.50	25	5.72
Total		**437**	**100.00**

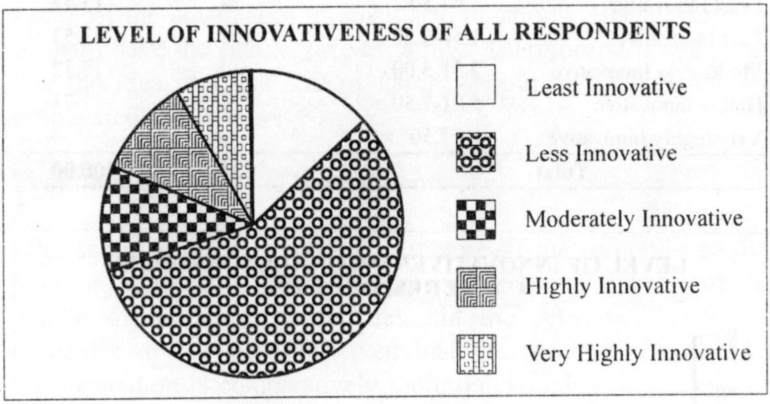

Fig. 4.11

The above analysis gives an aggregate picture of the level of innovativeness but there are a lot of inter-caste, rural-urban and scheduled caste and non-scheduled caste variations in it. Therefore, an in depth analysis has been done in the succeeding pages.

Level of Innovativeness of Scheduled Caste Respondents

Although there are 1112 scheduled caste respondents but only 231 which account roughly 21 percentage of the total scheduled caste respondents are engaged in farming activities (Table 4.41). The scrutiny of master table and detailed questionnaire of these respondents indicate that their size of holding is small, economic condition is poor and the agricultural infrastructure are almost at the lowest web. Hence, their level of innovativeness is low. More than 80 per cent of the respondents of this category have very low level of innovativeness (Fig.4.12). About 17 per cent of respondents belong to the moderate category while only 4 respondents contributing less than 2 per cent of the respondents of this category, belong to the highly innovativeness category. There is none in the category of very highly innovativeness.

Table 4.41 : Level of Innovativeness of All Scheduled Caste Respondents

Category	*Score Range*	*No. of Respondents*	*%age to total*
Least Innovative	<1.50	34	13.42
Less Innovative	1.50-2.50	156	67.53
Moderately Innovative	2.51-5.00	40	17.32
Highly Innovative	5.01-7.50	4	1.73
Very highly Innovative	>7.50	—	—
Total		**231**	**100.00**

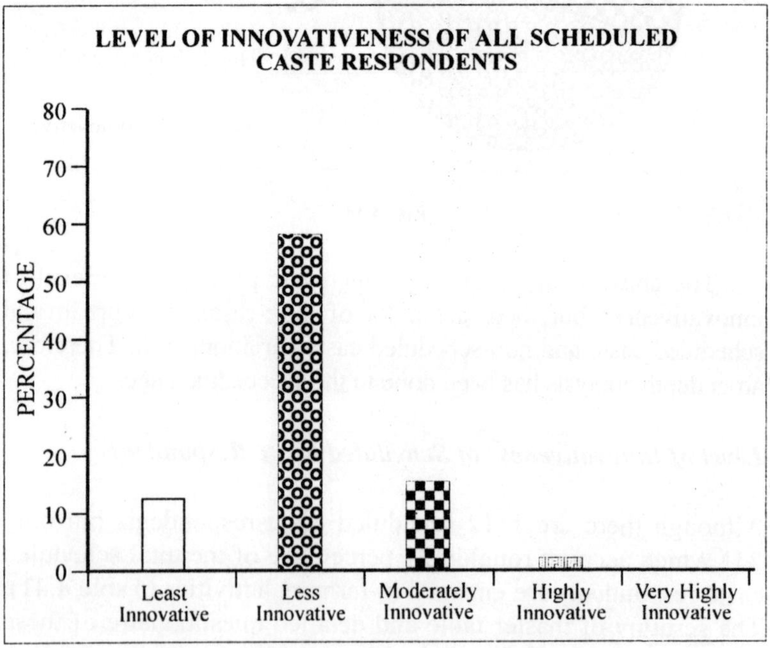

Fig. 4.12

There are variations in the level of innovativeness within the farming scheduled caste respondents. Among scheduled caste respondents, by and large, the urban scheduled castes are more innovative than the rural scheduled caste respondents who account roughly 87 per cent of the total farming scheduled caste respondents (Table 4.42). Out of which nearly 81 per cent belong to the lower category of innovativeness with innovative score of less than 2.5. Nearly 17 per cent of the respondents fall under the moderate category, while only 4 respondents amounting to 1.7 percent have high level of innovativeness.

Table 4.42 : Level of Innovativeness of Rural Scheduled Caste Respondents

Category	*Score Range*	*No. of Respondents*	*%age to total*
Least Innovative	<1.50	28	13.93
Less Innovative	1.50-2.50	136	67.66
Moderately Innovative	2.51-5.00	34	16.66
Highly Innovative	5.01-7.50	3	1.49
Very highly Innovative	>7.50	–	–
Total		**231**	**100.00**

As pointed out earlier the urban farming scheduled caste respondent have comparatively high level of innovativeness and nearly 23 per cent of the urban farming scheduled caste belong to the high category of innovativeness with innovation score of more than 5 (Table 4.43). Almost 10 per cent belong to the least innovativeness but nearly 67 per cent belong to the less category of innovativeness among urban farming scheduled castes. It is because of their high level of education, knowledge and involvement in agricultural activities. They are also more innovative.

Table 4.43 : Level of Innovativeness of Urban Scheduled Caste Respondents

Category	*Score range*	*No. of Respondents*	*%age to total*
Least Innovative	<1.50	3	10.00
Less Innovative	1.50-2.50	20	66.67
Moderate Innovative	2.51-5.00	6	20.00
Highly Innovative	5.01-7.50	1	3.33
Very Highly Innovative	>7.50	–	–
Total		**30**	**100.00**

The non-scheduled caste respondents which account roughly 26 per cent of the total respondents are, by and large, farmers. They own agricultural land and have better agricultural infrastructure. Their financial condition and the level of education is also higher. Therefore, they are more innovative than the farming scheduled caste respondents. Out of the total 397 non-scheduled castes, 206 amounting to 52 per cent belong to the farming category (Table 4.44). Out of this less than 10 per cent belong to least innovative category, while about 43 per cent are accounted to the less innovative categories. About 17 per cent of the non-scheduled caste farming respondents belong to each moderately and highly innovative category, while more than 12 per cent fall in the very highly innovative category.

Table 4.44 : Level of Innovativeness of All Non-Scheduled Caste Respondents

Category	*Score range*	*No. of Respondents*	*%age to total*
Least Innovative	<1.50	19	9.23
Less Innovative	1.50-2.50	89	43.21
Moderate Innovative	2.51-5.00	36	17.47
Highly Innovative	5.01-7.50	37	17.96
Very Highly Innovative	>7.50	25	12.13
Total		**206**	**100.00**

Table 4.45 : Level of Innovativeness of Rural Non-Scheduled Caste Respondents

Category	*Score range*	*No. of Respondents*	*%age to total*
Least Innovative	<1.50	18	9.52
Less Innovative	1.50-2.50	81	42.86
Moderate Innovative	2.51-5.00	33	17.46
Highly Innovative	5.01-7.50	34	17.99
Very Highly Innovative	>7.50	23	12.17
Total		**189**	**100.00**

There are differences in the level of innovativeness among the rural and urban non-scheduled caste farming respondents, which is evident from Tables 4.44 and 4.45. A close scrutiny of Table 4.45 indicates that the level of innovativeness of rural non-scheduled caste farming respondents is low. But when we look at the level of innovativeness of urban non-scheduled caste farming respondents we find that their level of innovativeness is comparatively much higher (Table 4.46). There is only one urban respondent who has least innovativeness, while 7 respondents amounting to nearly 41 per cent belong to the category of less innovativeness. There are about 30 per cent of the respondents who have a high level of innovativeness with more than five innovation scores. Slightly less than one-fourth of the respondents belong to moderate category. This statistical analysis reveals the fact that the urban population by virtue of having higher level of education, better infrastructural facilities, high degree of knowledge and involvement are more innovative.

Table 4.46 : Level of Innovativeness of Urban Non-Scheduled Caste Respondents

Category	*Score range*	*No. of Respondents*	*%age to total*
Least Innovative	<1.50	1	5.88
Less Innovative	1.50-2.50	7	41.18
Moderate Innovative	2.51-5.00	4	23.53
Highly Innovative	5.01-7.50	3	17.65
Very Highly Innovative	>7.50	2	11.76
Total		**17**	**100.00**

The close scrutiny of questionnaire of the farming respondents also indicates the rural-urban differential in the level of innovativeness. In general the rural respondent are less innovative as compared to the urban respondents (Tables 4.47 and 4.48). About 67 per cent of the rural respondents have lower level of innovativeness, while more than 17 per cent belong to moderate category. The category of high-level of innovativeness includes about 15 per cent of the total rural non-scheduled caste respondents which accounts 14 per cent of the total farming respondents. They have comparatively higher level of innovativeness which is inconformity with the earlier analysis. However, about 66 per cent of the urban respondents belong to the lower category of innovativeness, while nearly 13 per cent belong to the high category with an innovation score of more than 5.

Table 4.47 : Level of Innovativeness of All Rural Respondents

Category	*Score range*	*No. of Respondents*	*%age to total*
Least Innovative	<1.50	46	11.80
Less Innovative	1.50-2.50	217	55.64
Moderate Innovative	2.51-5.00	67	17.18
Highly Innovative	5.01-7.50	37	9.48
Very Highly Innovative	>7.50	23	5.90
Total		**390**	**100.00**

Table 4.48 : Level of Innovativeness of All Urban Respondents

Category	*Score range*	*No.of Respondents*	*%age to total*
Least Innovative	<1.50	4	8.51
Less Innovative	1.50-2.50	27	57.45
Moderate Innovative	2.51-5.00	10	21.27
Highly Innovative	5.01-7.50	4	8.51
Very Highly Innovative	>7.50	2	4.26
Total		**47**	**100.00**

The above analysis of level of innovativeness highlights the differential patterns of innovativeness among the various categories of respondents, which in turn have affected the overall socio-economic transformation of the population in general and the scheduled caste population in particular.

Occupational Diversification

The occupational structure of India's population in general and that of scheduled castes in particular has undergone a sea change during the last two decades. Agriculture has no longer remained the single, safe and remunerative occupation of the rural masses due to vagaries of weather conditions and technological advancement. Now agriculture or any other single occupation does not fulfil the requirements of the people. Therefore, they have diversified their activities and have adopted dairy farming, poultry, piggeries, fishing, labour, etc. as their main or subsidiary activity, because a single occupation many a times does not fulfil the necessities of their household. It is more so when the family is large and demands are varied. Therefore, not only the head of the household but also other senior members of the family go for several other occupations. Even the scheduled castes who were once branded as agricultural labourer, by and large, do not prefer to work in the agricultural fields alone mainly due to low wages and changed socio-economic order. They now prefer white-collar jobs in neighbouring towns or even distant cities.

Dairy Farming

Dairy farming has emerged as an important occupation. Sizeable number of scheduled caste and non-scheduled caste respondents have adopted it. Table 4.49 shows that altogether 194 respondents amounting to 12.8 per cent of the total are practicing dairy farming. It includes 173 rural and 21 urban respondents.

Table 4.49 : Dairy Farming Among Respondents

Nature	*Rural*	*Urban*	*Total*
A. Commercial	108	13	121
B. Subsistence	65	8	73
A. Main Income	23	5	28
B. Subsidiary Income	85	8	93

It is interesting to note that 121 are practicing it on commercial basis, while remaining 73 have adopted it on subsistence basis. The scrutiny of the questionnaire and the master table shows that large number of these respondents are scheduled castes. They have preferred dairy farming because of two reasons: *firstly,* the government provides loans and subsidies for it; and *secondly,* the socio-religious taboos of not using milk from a scheduled caste house has also loosened the grip. Initially they started selling milk through non-scheduled caste agents to distant or even local tea stalls but subsequently, they themselves started selling milk directly not only to tea stalls but to the households also. Table 4.49 further shows that dairy farming is the main source of income of 28 respondents (23 rural and 5 urban), while it is subsidiary source of income for 93 respondents. Another recent feature of dairy farming is that there are certain people with dairy farming as their hereditary occupation, who purchase the milk in the distant rural areas from dairy farmers of different castes (high and low or upper and lower) and resell it at higher prices in the urban centres.

Piggeries

Piggeries is another occupation which has gained importance only among scheduled caste respondents because of social and cultural factors. It has picked up mainly because of three reasons: *firstly,* they are getting financial incentives of different level from the government in the form of subsidies and loans; *secondly*, it has now become very lucrative occupation; and *thirdly,* various new breeds are provided by the government at cheaper cost.

Table 4.50 : Piggeries Farming Among Respondents

Nature	*Rural*	*Urban*	*Total*
A. Commercial	75	16	91
B. Subsistence	8	7	15
A. Main Income	62	8	70
B. Subsidiary Income	13	8	21

Table 4.50 shows that 106 scheduled caste respondents amounting to 9.53 per cent of the total scheduled caste respondents are practicing piggeries. Out of this 83 respondents (78%) belong to rural areas and remaining 23 (22%) are urban respondents. The other interesting result emerging from Table 4.49 is that 91 respondents covering about 86 per cent of the total practice it on commercial basis, while 15 respondents (14%) are doing it on subsistence basis. The other glaring inference is that 70 respondents amounting to 77 per cent of total respondents have it as main source of their income, while for 21 respondents covering about 23 per cent respondents, it is subsidiary form of income.

Fishing

Fishing is another alternative occupation which has attracted 185 respondents from both rural and urban areas. In fact, only 4 respondents belong to urban areas and remaining 181 are rural respondents (Table 4.51).

Table 4.51 : Fishing Among Respondents

Nature	*Rural*	*Urban*	*Total*
A. Commercial	68	-	68
B. Subsistence	113	4	117
A. Main Income	6		6
B. Subsidiary Income	62	-	62

It is more popular in the rural areas because: *firstly,* there are plenty of water bodies both perennial and non-perennial in the rural areas which provide space for breeding and rearing of fish; and *secondly,* the rural people are not only more interested in it as their hobby but have more time to devote towards this profession. However, majority of the respondents (63%) practice it on subsistence basis, while only 68 respondents (37%) are doing it on commercial basis. Out of this, 6 have expressed it as their main source of income, while 62 respondents are doing it to supplement their income. However, looking at the water bodies (ponds, lakes, rivers) in the state, it may be safely said that this occupation has a huge potential and the government should encourage it by providing various kind of incentives and subsidies.

Poultry Farming

Poultry farming is not a popular economic activity because of the socio-cultural taboos. The state is dominantly inhabited by the Hindu population who are, by and large, vegetarian in their dietary habits. As such only 33 respondents including 27 rural and 6 urban, were practicing poultry farming. Nearly 82 per cent respondents are rural and most of them are Muslims (Table 4.52).

Table 4.52 : Poultry Farming Among Respondents

Nature	*Rural*	*Urban*	*Total*
A. Commercial	27	6	33
B. Subsistence	9	11	20
A. Main Income	4	2	6
B. Subsidiary Income	23	4	27

In the recent past scheduled caste population has also started poultry farming partly on the commercial and partly on subsistence basis. It is a poor man's occupation which he does in order to supplement his household income. Out of 53 respondents, 33 are practicing it on commercial basis. But it is the main source of income of only 6 respondents and for remaining 27 it is subsidiary source of income.

Labour

Labour has been the main occupation of the masses of the rural India in general and scheduled castes in particular. Even today, out of the total of 1510, 986 respondents (65%) are engaged in this occupation because neither they have the land to cultivate nor the capital to go for a small household industry or a little business, nor they have requisite education to be absorbed in service. A substantial number of labourer respondents (742 out of 986) live in rural areas. Earlier majority of them used to be engaged in contract labour for a fixed period of time which is normally one agricultural year. In lieu they were getting about one-sixth of the agricultural product and 2-3 bigha of agricultural land. Now, due to agricultural modernization and a little more awakening among the labourers this practice has almost ceased. Now the labourer prefer free lancing work in any sector anywhere if it is more lucrative. The recent trend is that they take work of any kind anywhere within their commutable reach on contract basis. Either they have their almost permanent homogeneous group or they form the group as and when it is required and accomplish the contract work. It is more lucrative to the labourer and tension free to the employer. The only negative aspect is that the quality of work suffers if the employer is not vigilant.

Besides these, white-collar job (service) is gaining popularity. Due to increasing level of education and comparatively more opening for jobs, the number of respondents in service of various kinds is increasing. The urban respondents are more in service than the rural ones. Almost equal number of scheduled caste and non-scheduled caste respondents are in service. There are very few respondents whose main source of livelihood is service. In substantial number of cases, one or two members of the family are in service mostly within the commuting distance from their village. In very few cases the person in job lives outside his village and even, if he does, mostly be lives alone leaving his family in the village. In addition to these, 191 respondents including 141 rural and 50 urban are engaged in numerous occupations too many to mention them individually here.

The above analysis clearly shows that the masses are diversifying their occupation, and they prefer the lucrative ones to increase their socio-economic status.

REFERENCES

Bhatia, B.M.,1977: *Poverty, Agriculture and Economic Growth,* Vikas, New Delhi.

Bose, S.P., 1961: Characteristics of Farmers Who Adopt Agricultural Practices in Indian Villages, *Rural Sociology*, Vol.26.

Brown, L.R.,1971: *Social Impact of Green Revolution,* Coarnegie, New York.

Desai, D.K., 1966: Technological Change and its Diffusion in Agriculture, *Indian Journal of agricultural Economics*, No. I, Vol. XXI.

Lees, E.S.,1966: A Theory of Migration, *Demography*, Vol. 3.

Mohammad, N., and Pathania, A.,1997: 'Spatial Inequality in Man-Land Ratio in India' in Akhtar, R.(ed.) *Contemporary Approaches to Indian Geography*, APH Pub., Delhi.

Mohammad, N.,1978 : 'Impact of Social Factors on Diffusion of Agricultural Innovation in Central Trans-Ghaghara Plain'. *National Geographical Journal of India*, Vol. XXIV, Varanasi.

Rangaswamy, P., *et al.*,1972: *India's Changing Farmers,* Allahabad.

Rani, U., 1971: 'Farm Size and Productivity', *Economic and Political Weekly*, June, pp. A 85-A 89.

Raza, M.,1992 : *Development and Ecology,* Rawat Publications, Jaipur.

Sharma, A.C., 1976: *Mechanisation of Punjab Agriculture*, New Delhi.

Sharma, K.L., 1972: Levels of Mobility in Caste Structure. 'A Hypothetical Refinement', *The Indian Journal of Social Work*, Vol. XXXII, No. 4.

Shetty, M.S.,1966: Inter-Farm Rate of Technological Diffusion in Indian Agriculture, *Indian Journal of Agricultural Economics,* Vol. XXI.

Singh, J., 1974 : *The Green Revolution in India —How Green it is*? Kurukshetra.

Wilkening, E.H., 1950: A Socio-Psychological Approach to the Study of Acceptance of Innovations in Farming, *Rural Sociology*.

5

LEVEL OF SOCIAL TRANSFORMATION

Ever since independence India has formulated and implemented various programmes and policies through its various Five Year Plans for the social upliftment of the masses in general and scheduled castes in particular. The government has introduced the programme of free primary education, scholarship to scheduled castes and backward castes, mid-day meal, free distribution of foodgrains, sale of foodgrains at much lower prices to weaker section, family welfare programme, various incentives to adoption of family planning programmes and many other similar programmes from time to time for the social upliftment of the weaker section of the society. As a result there has been considerable changes in various social parameters of the people in general and the scheduled castes in particular. Among various social parameters changing age composition of respondents involved in decision making process in family affairs, educational level, and family size have already been discussed in Chapter 4 dealing with socio-economic structure of respondents, rules to the changing attitude of the respondents towards education, marriage, family planning, religion, political awareness and involvement and social mobility have been considered here. A brief account of each of these social parameters is given here.

Attitude Towards Education

The importance of education in the process of socio-economic transformation has already been discussed in the earlier chapter, which indicates a positive sign of improvement of the literacy level. It has also become quite obvious that the literacy level among younger generation is more than the older ones which is a very encouraging feature. It has been observed that the rural people including the scheduled castes have high ambitions and aspirations regarding not only the education of their children but also their jobs. Therefore, an attempt has been made to find out the preferences of the parents regarding the nature and locations of the schools for their children. Attempt has also been made to make queries regarding the preferences of the job of their son and daughter in certain selected categories of jobs. Based on the responses of the respondents a brief analysis pertaining to the (i) Preference of the location of the school (within village); (ii) Preference of the location of the school (outside the village); and (iii) Preference of the job of the children is presented here.

Preference of the Location of School (Within Village)

Preference of the location of the school is a good indicator of the urge, desire and ambition of the parents for the education of their children. It has been observed that generally the parents prefer a school, which is very easily accessible irrespective of its quality. But the parents who are concerned about quality education prefer to send their children outside the village or even to the towns and cities in search of quality education. With this perspective a tabular questionnaire pertaining to the education of their both male and female children for primary, secondary, senior secondary, and higher education in government school and public school within the village or outside the village including towns and cities was included in the survey schedule. The results have been given in Tables 5.1, 5.2 and 5.3.

Table 5.1 : Preferences of Location of School of Total Respondents for Children (Within Village)

Preferences	*Children*	*No. of Respondents*	*%age to total*
Govt. School	(a) Daughter	1033	46.59
	(b) Son	1026	46.28
Public School	(a) Daughter	78	3.52
	(b) Son	80	3.61
Total		**2217**	**100.00**

While processing the questionnaire regarding the preference of location of school for the education of the children it was found that 156 respondents have not responded while 647 respondents have responded either for son or for daughter. There are 863 respondents who have given their preferences for both. As such the total number does not tally with the actual total and it goes to 2217. Out of this 2059 have preferred government schools for their sons (1033) and daughters (1026) education, while 158 respondents covering 7 per cent of the total have preferred public schools for the education of their children within the village (Fig.5.1). The statistical analysis presents several interesting and encouraging results: *firstly,* the parents are now not only concerned about the education of their children but they prefer quality education by sending their children to public school; *secondly,* they are almost equally concerned with the quality education for their daughters; *thirdly,* they are willing to spend money on the quality education of their children; and *finally*, in the lower standards, viz. primary and middle, the preference is more for public schools.

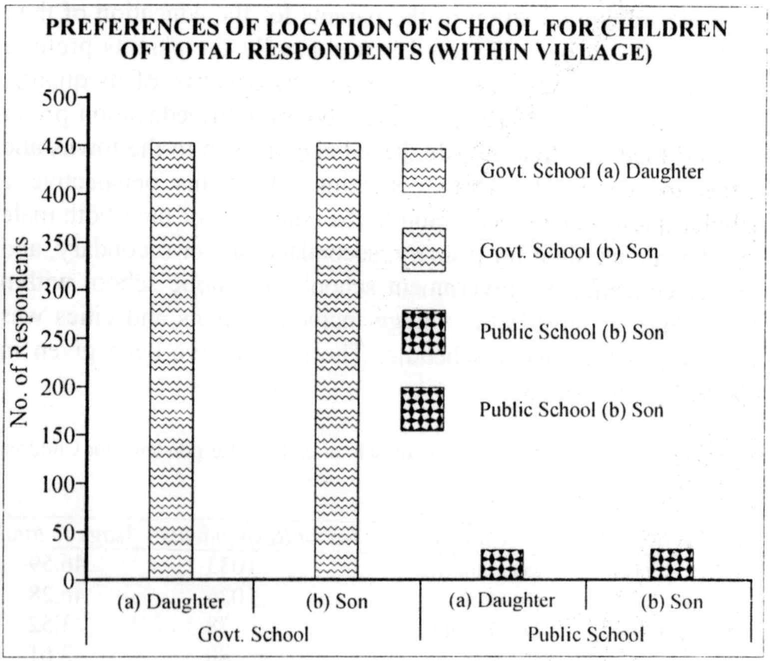

Fig. 5.1

The above analysis represents the aggregate picture of all respondents but there is rural-urban differential in the preferences. Out of 1614 rural respondents 1520 respondents amounting to 94 per cent of the total have preferences for government schools within the village for their children in all standards of education, while 94 respondents covering 5 per cent of the total have expressed their desire to educate their children in public schools within the village (Table 5.2).

Table 5.2 : Preferences of Location of School of Rural Respondent for Children (within village)

Preferences	*Children*	*No. of Respondents*	*%age to total*
Govt. School	(a) Daughter	766	47.46
	(b) Son	754	46.72
Public School	(a) Daughter	46	2.85
	(b) Son	48	2.97
Total		**1614**	**100.00**

The preference of urban respondents has been shown in Table 5.3, which shows that there are altogether 603 responses of urban respondents for both daughters and sons. Out of this nearly 89 per cent have preferred government school for their children within the village, while 64 respondents covering about 11 per cent of the total have shown their desire to send their children to public schools.

Table 5.3 : Preferences of Location of School of Urban Respondent for Children (within village)

Preferences	*Children*	*No. of Respondents*	*%age to total*
Govt. School	(a) Daughter	267	44.27
	(b) Son	272	45.11
Public School	(a) Daughter	32	5.31
	(b) Son	32	5.31
Total		**603**	**100.00**

Table 5.3 further shows that there is hardly any discrimination between son and daughter regarding the preference of the school for their education. And, it is a very strong positive sign of social transformation.

Preference of Location of Schools (outside the village)

The aspiration for the education of the children may be even stronger if they prefer to send their children outside their place of residence. It is generally observed that if the parents send their children for education outside their locality, it is very strong proof of their desire of the higher and quality education. With this perspective another tabular set of questionnaire was set up to find out the preferences of the parents regarding the education of their children including son and daughter for various standards outside the village. The questionnaires have been processed and the results have been shown in Tables 5.4, 5.5 and 5.6.

Table 5.4 : Preferences of Location of School of All Respondent for Children (Outside Village)

Preferences	*Children*	*No. of Respondents*	*%age to total*
Govt. School	(a) Daughter	77	37.56
	(b) Son	94	45.85
Public School	(a) Daughter	16	7.81
	(b) Son	18	8.78
Total		**205**	**100.00**

It is obvious from Table 5.4 that only 205 respondents covering about 14 per cent of the total respondents have given their preferences regarding the education of their children outside the village. Out of this 171 covering about 83 per cent of the respondents under this category show their desire to educate their

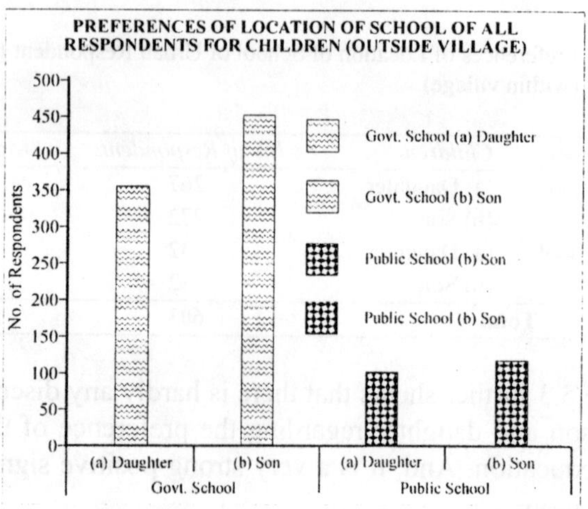

Fig. 5.2

they are more open to send their sons outside the village than the daughters, which stands to reason that it is more risky and problematic to send daughters outside the village. About 16 per cent of the respondents have shown their desire to educate their children in the public school outside the village. In this case the difference among the son and daughter is not very glaring. This is because of the fact that in majority of the public schools there is a residential facility. Hence, it makes little difference whether you send the son or the daughter to these public schools. Another interesting feature also emerges when we compare the total number of preferences with reference to boys and girls. It is in fact very nominal. The above discussion very clearly proves the high desire of the parents to educate their children even if they are sending outside the village. It is a clear sign of social transformation.

Table 5.5 shows the rural-urban differentials in preferences of the localities regarding the education of children. It indicates the choices of the rural respondents. It shows that 171 respondents covering about 86 per cent of the total respondents under this category prefer to educate their children in the government school outside the village.

Table 5.5 : Preferences of Location of School of Rural Respondent for Children (Outside Village)

Preferences	*Children*	*No. of Respondents*	*%age to total*
Govt. School	(a) Daughter	77	38.50
	(b) Son	94	47.00
Public School	(a) Daughter	13	6.50
	(b) Son	16	8.00
Total		**200**	**100.00**

Table 5.5 further shows that the preferences for the female child education is also quite high amounting to about 47 per cent of the respondents falling under this category. Twenty-nine respondents covering about 14 per cent to total have shown their preferences for public school outside the village. The analysis shows that there is a sea change in the attitude of the respondents regarding the education and preferences of the localities. The

parents do not mind in sending their, even their female child outside village for better and quality education. As regards the urban respondents the preference of the school outside the localities is not very high because these localities themselves have better educational facilities. Only 5 urban respondents have shown their desire to educate their children outside their town, perhaps, because of the fact that the facilities for higher education are not available in their towns.

In the preceding discussion differences in the levels of various educational parameters have been discussed and explained but all these parameters are of different nature and character and cannot be aggregated and averaged in their original forms. Hence, a weighted scheme of scores has been followed and results are presented in Table 5.6 which shows that 1308 respondents

Table 5.6 : Index of Educational Status

Category	*Score Range*	*No. of Respondents*	*%age to total*
High	More than 3.50	65	4.30
Medium	3.50-2.50	137	9.07
Low	Less than 2.50	1308	86.63
	Total	**1510**	**100.00**

amounting to about 87 per cent fall in the low category. Out of the remaining 13 per cent nearly 9 per cent belong to medium category and 4 per cent to high category. This clearly indicates that inspite of all incentives and encouragements the overall index of education have not increased a higher level.

Preference of the Job for Children

With the increasing aspiration of the parents regarding the quality of education their preferences for the jobs of their children has also undergone a sea change. In the recent past they were aspiring for their children to be almost a constable *(Sipahi)* or a *SHO (Daroga)*. They use to bless their children to be a *Sipahi* or a *Daroga* which reveals height of their ambition which has undergone a change. Now they aspire them to be a doctor, engineer and an officer of a high rank. With this back log a number of questions were included to assess their attitudes regarding the jobs of their children. The processed data is represented

Table 5.7 : Preferences of All Respondent for Job of Children

Children	*Jobs Preferences*					
	Doctor	*Engineer*	*Civil Servant*	*Lawyer*	*Teacher*	*Other*
Son	162	137	89	128	169	604
Daughter	270	13	15	9	381	588
Total	**432**	**150**	**104**	**137**	**550**	**1192**

in Table 5.7 which indicates that 432 respondents accounting to 36.24 per cent of total respondents have desired their children to be a doctor. The preference for the medical profession is more for the female children than the male ones. It is 62.5 per cent for the former, while 37.5 per cent to the latter (Fig. 5.3).

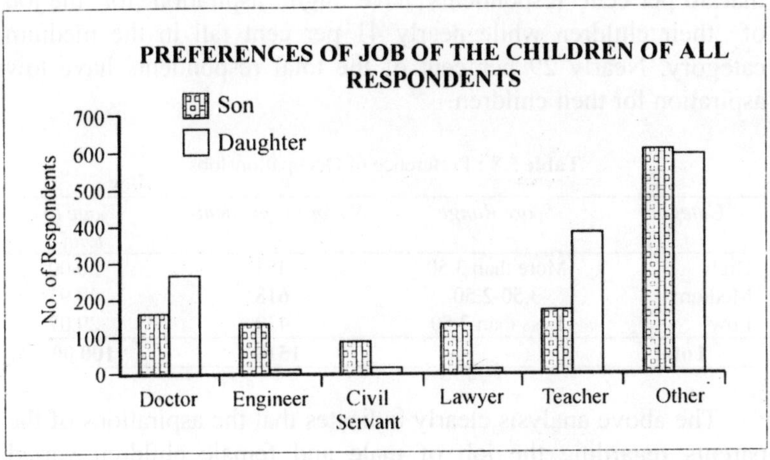

Fig. 5.3

Contrary is true in case of technical profession for which 130 respondents amounting to 91 per cent of total have opted it for their sons and only 13 respondents amounting to 9 per cent have favoured this profession for their female child. Nearly 7 per cent respondents have opted civil services as the job of their children. Out of which 85.60 per cent have opted for their sons and 14.4 per cent for their daughters. Almost similar proportions have been expressed regarding the lawyer as the profession of their children which covers about 9 per cent of the total respondents. The teaching profession have been observed to be most popular and acceptable. Nearly 36 per cent respondents have expressed their desire of a teacher for their children. The teaching profession has been preferred more for the female children (69%) than the male (31%).

However, there are inter and intra rural-urban variations in the job preferences for the children. The common view which emerges from the scrutiny of questionnaire is that the urban respondents, by and large, have better preferences than their rural counterpart.

As the nature of the jobs and the responses received from the respondents were of different nature and kind, it was not possible to aggregate them. Hence, a weighted scheme of scores has been followed and results are represented in Table 5.8 which shows that 30 per cent respondents have high aspiration for the job of their children while nearly 41 per cent fall in the medium category. Nearly 29 per cent of the total respondents have low aspiration for their children.

Table 5.8 : Preference of Occupation/Jobs

Category	*Score Range*	*No. of Respondents*	*%age to total*
High	More than 3.50	453	30.00
Medium	3.50-2.50	618	40.93
Low	Less than 2.50	439	29.07
Total		**1510**	**100.00**

The above analysis clearly indicates that the aspirations of the parents regarding the job of male and female children varied according to nature of job. Generally the soft jobs are preferred for the female child, while the harder ones are preferred for the male children.

Attitude Towards Marriage

Marriage is a socio-religious bond among the people of the opposite sex and is normally expected to remain intact till the termination of life. In the past there were many superstitions, misbelieves and traditional and orthodox viewpoints about various parameters of marriage but now the whole marriage system is in the process of change. The attitude towards various aspects of marriage such as child marriage, widow marriage, widowhood, re-marriage, love marriage and inter-caste marriage has undergone a major change. Various rituals of marriage have not only changed but have become more simple and modernised. The overall response of the scheduled castes is towards the positive change. They are becoming more liberal and more receptive to modern ideologies. The process of change has been set in motion and it may pick-up very soon.

However, in order to assess the change in the attitude of the respondents towards the marriage several indicators such as age at marriage, nature of marriage, distance of marriage, process of marriage, dowry system etc. have been taken into consideration. The responses of the respondents have been recorded and the brief summary of the same is presented below.

Age at marriage is one of the important parameters in the consideration of attitude towards marriage. In the past the marriages among the masses in general and the weaker section in particular used to take place in the childhood which had its own several limitations and disadvantages. In some conditions the marriages were decided even before the birth of the child. However, there has been a positive change regarding the age at marriage. People have not only started thinking but also arranging the marriages of their children in the age group of 20-30 years. Based on the response of the respondents the analysis of the preferences of age at marriage and the actual age at the marriage in practice has been analysed.

Table 5.9 shows the preferences of the age at the marriage in which 1481 respondents have recorded their preferences regarding the age of the marriage of their sons. It is interesting to note that 66 respondents amounting to roughly 4.5 per cent of the total have preferred to get their sons married at the age of more than 25 years, whereas about 87 per cent of the respondents have shown their preference of 18-25 years as the age of marriage of their sons (Fig.5.4). As such around 92 per cent respondents have preferred more than 18 years of the age for the marriage of their sons which

Table 5.9 : Preferences of All Respondents of the Age at Marriage for Boys

Preferred Years	*No. of Respondents*	*%age to total*
>25 Years	66	4.46
18-25 Years	1293	87.31
<18 Years	122	8.23
Total	**1481**	**100.00**

is very good sign of positive social transformation. About 8 per cent of the total respondents, of which most of them are old age respondents have preferred less than 18 years age for the marriage of their sons.

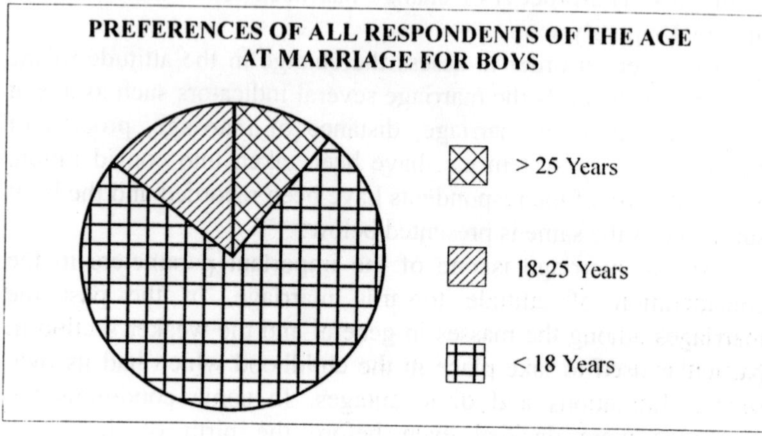

Fig. 5.4

A close scrutiny of master table and the questionnaire indicates that there are rural-urban differentials in the preference of age at marriage. By and large, lesser number of rural people has preferred higher age for the marriage of their sons as compared to the urban respondents. In case of rural respondents about 89 per cent have preferred more than 18 years of age and 10 per cent for less than 18 years, while in case of urban respondents the corresponding percentages are roughly 99 per cent and one per cent respectively.

The preference of age at the marriage for the female child is different from the male child. It has been observed that the respondents prefer lower age for the marriage of their daughter across the board. Table 5.10 showing the age preference for the female child indicates that 7 per cent respondents prefer more than

Table 5.10 : Preferences of All Respondents of the Age at Marriage for Girls

Preference Years	*No. of Respondents*	*%age to total*
>25 Years	105	7.09
15-25 Years	1286	86.89
<15 Years	89	6.02
Total	**1480**	**100.00**

20 years of the age for girl child, while around 87 per cent has reported between 15 and 20 years of age. As such a total of 94 per cent have opted for higher age for their girl child, while only 6 per cent have preferred less than 15 years age for the same (Fig.5.5). In this case also there is difference between rural and urban respondents. About 92 per cent of the rural respondents have opted more than 15 years as age of the marriage for their girl child and only 8 per cent have preferred less than 15 years, whereas the corresponding figure in case of urban respondents is more than 99 per cent and less than one per cent respectively.

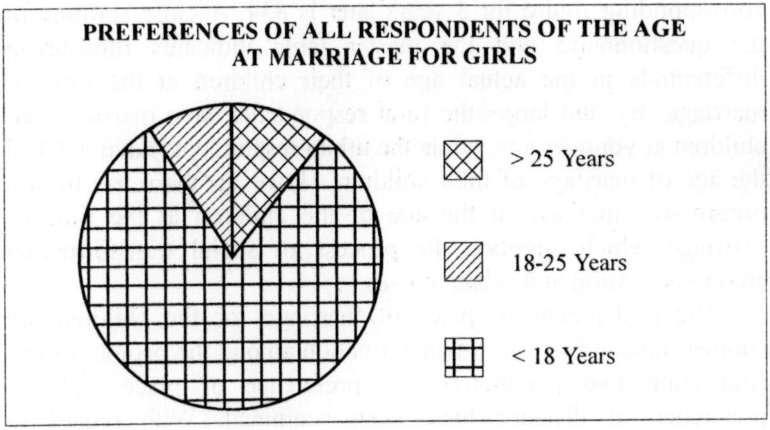

Fig. 5.5

With the process of social transformation the age at marriage has kept on changing. Social capillary theory of population growth has become more operative. People delay their marriages for attaining higher social status by gaining more economic prosperity. In order to assess it questions pertaining to the age at marriage 5 years before and 10 years before were included in the questionnaire. The processed result has been given in Table 5.11, which represents the strong positive change in the age at the marriage. It is observed that 10 years before only 9 respondents amounting to less than one per cent had married their children after 20 years of age, while 5 years later the corresponding number in the same age group has gone up to 110 covering about 7.5 per cent of the total respondents. On the contrary the number of respondents marrying their children at the age of less than 15 years was 604 which have reduced to 536 in the corresponding age group.

Table 5.11 : Age at Marriage of the Children of All Respondents

Age Group	*10 Years Before*		*5 Years Before*	
	No. of Respondents	*%age to total*	*No. of Respondents*	*%age to total*
>20 Years	9	0.65	110	7.43
15-20 Years	767	55.58	834	56.35
<15 Years	604	43.77	536	36.22
Total	**1380**	**100.00**	**1480**	**100.00**

Similarly in the age group of 15 to 20 years 767 respondents have married their children 10 years before, while the corresponding figure for 5 years later is 834. A close scrutiny of the questionnaire and the master table indicates rural-urban differentials in the actual age of their children at the time of marriage. By and large, the rural respondents have married their children at younger age, while the urban respondents have delayed the age of marriage of their children. However, there has been a progressive increase in the age of the children at the time of marriage which supports the process of social transformation among both rural and urban masses.

The preferences of place of marriage for the children are another indicator of social transformation among the people. In this connection two parameters, i.e. preference of place and the preference of distance have been examined. With regard to preference of place it has been found that nearly 53 per cent of the reported respondents in this category prefer the village for the marriage of their children (Table 5.12). Majority of these respondents belong to the villages but there are quite a few who prefer the villages for the marriage of their children although they are settled in towns and cities. This is because of the fact that they are recent migrants in the city and they have very strong root in their

Table 5.12 : Preferences of Place of Marriage of all Respondents

Preferential Place	*No. of Person*	*%age to total*
Village	797	53.17
Town	371	24.75
City	83	5.54
Village & Town	203	13.54
Others	45	3.00
Total	**1499**	**100.00**

village. A little less than one-fourth of the total respondents have preferred town, while about 6 per cent have opted city as a place of marriage of their children (Fig.5.6). Majority of this belong to town and cities. There are about 14 per cent respondents who have opted for both village and town while 45 respondents amounting to 3 per cent have not specified the place of marriage for their children. As such about 17 per cent of respondent of this category have an open choice of the place of marriage of children which is again a sign of social transformation.

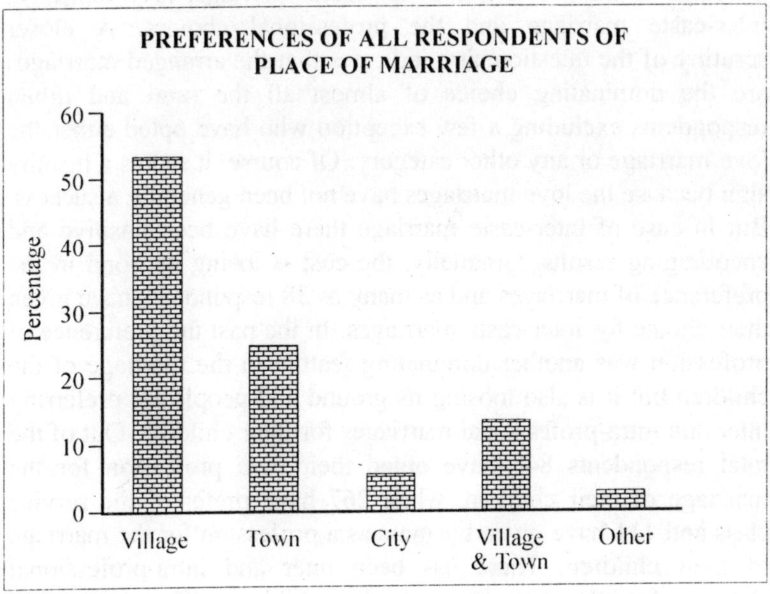

Fig. 5.6

In the past the people used to prefer a closer distance for the marriage of their children mainly because of the lack of means of transportation and socio-cultural affinity. But with the passage of time their social mobility has increased and the development of means of transport has facilitated their movement for a longer distance. Therefore, it has been found that the respondents prefer the match for their children on the basis of qualities and character rather than on distance. It has been observed that 10 years before majority of the respondents preferred to marry their children within a distance of 10 km which was the formidable distance for their movement. It has been observed from the master table and the questionnaire that after 5 years the number of respondents has preferred more than 10 kilometres of distance for marriage of their children if the match is good. Another interesting feature is that a large number of respondents have expressed their opinion that distance is no bar for the marriage of their children provided the match is good. All these indicate the sign of social transformation.

Another indicator of social transformation regarding the marriage is the preference of arranged marriage, love marriage, inter-caste marriage and the professional choices. A closer scrutiny of the questionnaire indicates that the arranged marriages are the dominating choice of almost all the rural and urban respondents excluding a few exception who have opted either the love marriage or any other category. Of course, it seems a healthy sign because the love marriages have not been generally a success. But in case of inter-caste marriage there have been positive and encouraging results. Gradually, the cost is losing its bond in the preference of marriages and as many as 38 respondents have given their choice for inter-caste marriages. In the past the preference of profession was another dominating feature in the marriage of the children but it is also loosing its ground and people are preferring inter and intra-professional marriages for their children. Out of the total respondents 845 have opted their own profession for the marriage of their children, while 267 have preferred the service class and 111 have given business as a profession for the marriage of their children. There has been inter and intra-professional choices for the marriage of the children. There are 163 respondents who have opted their own profession and the service, while 41 respondents have opted either service or business as a profession for their children. The interesting inference which could be drawn is that the people prefer the match who is economically well off and has a bright future.

Dowry is another menace in the Indian social system. In spite of various rules and legislations the dowry system has not minimised over the years. The questions pertaining to the assessment of dowry system in the past as well as at present for the marriage of male and female children were framed. On the basis of the information provided by the respondents it emerges that, by and large, dowry system is increasing with the passage of time. Although 1004 respondents have reported the prevalence of dowry system among their castes and 491 have given a negative answer, but the dowry system is prevalent among almost all the respondents. The parents of the girl child have to pay more today than 10 years before.

Various parameters of marriage have been discussed in detail in the preceding pages, but these parameters are not comparable with one another. Hence, a weighted score have been given to them. Based on this, the respondents have been classified into three categories (Table 5.13).

Table 5.13 : Index of Attitude Towards Marriage

Category	*Score Range*	*No of Respondent*	*%age to total*
High	>3.50	478	31.66
Medium	3.50-2.50	522	34.57
Low	>2.50	510	33.77
Total		**1510**	**100.00**

Table 5.13 shows almost uniform distribution of respondents in each category. There are 478 respondents amounting to about 32 per cent in high category which is the representative of more liberal, educated and advanced respondents. The respondents belonging to moderate category account about 35 per cent of the total, while 34 per cent fall in the low category.

Attitude Towards Family Planning

The explosive rate of growth of population is considered to be the greatest menace in the process of development of our country. And, therefore, various measures which have not been uniformly adopted by the people of all castes, have been suggested to curb the population growth. Earlier the rural masses, specially the scheduled castes, had conservative approach regarding the size of family. They considered large size family as a measure for social security and instrument for generating economic pursuits. According to them children are the gift of nature and any measure to prevent it is really a sin. But the younger and educated section of the scheduled castes are changing their structure and system of the family. Since it is linked with religion and economic gain, it will take comparatively longer time to change but the process has been set in motion.

However, for the assessment of the attitude of the respondents towards family planning programme a number of questions related to awareness, mode, attitude and adoption have been included in the questionnaire. A close look at the questionnaire reveals many interesting results. *Firstly,* although all the respondents have not responded to this questions but more than 90 per cent have responded except in case of its adoption. Nearly 64 per cent respondents are aware of the family planning programme. It includes both rural (690) and urban (282) respondents. Nearly 36 per cent respondents have shown their ignorance about family planning programme. Out of these majority of them belong to rural areas. *Secondly,* the respondents are not only aware of it but they are in favour of its adoption. A total of 815 including 641 urban and 174 rural respondents are in favour of adoption of family planning programme, while 684 (492 rural and 192 urban) have expressed their resentment in adoption of family planning programme. *Thirdly,* 1166 respondents have expressed their negative view regarding the large size of family for the economic development. The proportion of rural and urban respondents is almost the same. *Fourthly,* 1203 respondents including 876 rural and 327 urban have given their positive views regarding the small size of family. Both the views go in favour of family planning. *Fifthly,* out of 815 respondents favouring the adoption of family planning programme 500 including 392 rural and 108 urban respondents have adopted it. It is roughly 61 per cent of the total respondents which is a very strong positive sign towards the acceptance of family planning programme among almost all the respondents. *Sixthly,* regarding the choice of the sex for the adoption of family planning programme 873 respondents have favoured female adoption, while 623 have expressed their view in favour of male adoption. It clearly reflects the gender biasness because of the fact that the existing social system is as such in which males can do something else in case of any untoward happenings to female. The statistical analysis clearly indicates that the family planning programme is becoming popular among both rural and urban masses. However, the degree of adoption is more among urban respondents, than their counterpart.

The family planning programme, its adaptation and impact are very sensitive cultural issues. Therefore, in the formulation of the questionnaire utmost care has been taken so that it does not hurt their feelings, norms and values. Since the nature of the questions and their response was of different nature, it was not possible to aggregate the data. Hence, weighted scores have been given to responses of the respondents, and accordingly they have been grouped into three categories (Table 5.14).

Table 5.14 : Index of Family Planning

Category	*Score Range*	*No. of Respondent*	*%age of Total*
High	More than 3.50	261	18.61
Medium	3.50-2.50	473	31.32
Low	Less than 2.50	756	50.07
	Total	**1510**	**100.00**

It is evident from Table 5.14 that about half of the respondents are at a lower web in case of adoption of family planning programmes. It shows their strong bonds with rituals, traditions, customs and religion. However, there is hope of adoption of this programme because a little less than one-third respondents belong to medium category, while about 19 per cent are in the higher category. A scrutiny of master table shows that most of the respondents in the higher category are the educated younger generation respondents.

Level of Religiosity

Religion is a very important social indicator which provides a very strong bond of social fabric among the masses especially in Indian context. It has a very deep root in Indian social system and has a strong bearing on various other social parameters. In the past all the events in the society were attributed to religion. Various kind of superstitions and misbeliefs were there. Religion has a very strong bearing on the economic activity of the people too. But gradually with the increasing level of education the attitude towards religion is changing. People are becoming more liberal, less superstitious and less orthodox. They are now more receptive to new ideas and practices.

Since religion is a very complex, delicate, sensitive and touchy social element, its quantitative measurement is slightly difficult. However, a number of value-loaded and simple questions were put to the respondents of different socio-economic strata. Some of the important questions were related with religious beliefs, practices and its periodicity, superstitions, *Janampatri,* belief in natural calamities and disasters. A close look of the responses of the respondents and the master table indicates that there are a lot of changes in the religiosity of both the scheduled caste and non-scheduled caste respondents.

As the questions were of different nature and character, a weighted scoring scheme has been used to bring the various elements of religion comparable.

Scoring Scheme of Religiosity

(1) Do you believe in religion?

(1) Somewhat	:	0.15
(2) Moderately	:	0.30
(3) Strictly	:	0.45

(2) Do you follow the religious rules in your routine life?

(1) Somewhat	:	0.15
(2) Greatly	:	0.30
(3) Strictly	:	0.45

(3) Do you worship regularly as per religious rules?

(1) Yes	:	0.25
(2) No	:	0.00

(4) Do you visit religious places outside your village?

(1) Never	:	0.00
(2) Rarely	:	0.25
(3) Frequently	:	0.30

(5) Do you offer special pooja before taking up new jobs?

(1) Yes	:	0.20
(2) No	:	0.00

(6) Do you worship more at the time of hardship and distress?

(1) Yes : 0.20
(2) No : 0.00

(7) Do you believe in religious superstitions?

(1) Yes : 0.20
(2) No : 0.00

(8) Do you attend village religious functions?

(1) Never : 0.00
(2) Rarely : 0.15
(3) Frequently : 0.20

(9) Do you go about Janampatri in deciding about?

(a) Marriage:

(1) Yes : 0.10
(2) No : 0.00

(b) Marriage timings:

(1) Yes : 0.10
(2) No : 0.00

(c) Adoption of new jobs?

(1) Yes : 0.10
(2) No : 0.00

(10) Do you consult the Priest/religious head on special occasions in the family?

(1) Never : 0.00
(2) Rarely : 0.10
(3) Frequently : 0.20
(4) Always : 0.30

(11) Do you think that the calamities in our life are result of our KARAM in the past and present Life?

(1) Yes : 0.25
(2) No : 0.00

(12) Do you think that all disasters come from God?

(1) Yes : 0.25
(2) No : 0.00

(13) Is there any separate place of worship in your house?

(1) Yes : 0.20

(2) No : 0.00

According to this scoring scheme, scores have been given to each respondent, and their total religious scores have been worked out. On the basis of their total religious scores, they have arranged in ascending order and grouped into 4 categories (Table 5.15).

Table 5.15 : Level of Religiosity of All Respondents

Religious Group	Score Range	No. of Respondents	%age to total
Least Religious	<1.25	319	21.13
Less Religious	1.25-2.00	312	20.66
Moderately Religious	2.01-2.50	284	18.81
Highly Religious	>2.50	598	39.60
Total		**1510**	**100.00**

A cursory glance at Table 5.15 shows an overall change in the level of religiosity of all the categories of respondents. Out of 1510 respondents 300 have reported change in their level of religiosity, while the remaining 1210 have either not responded to these questions or have mentioned no change (Fig.5.7). More

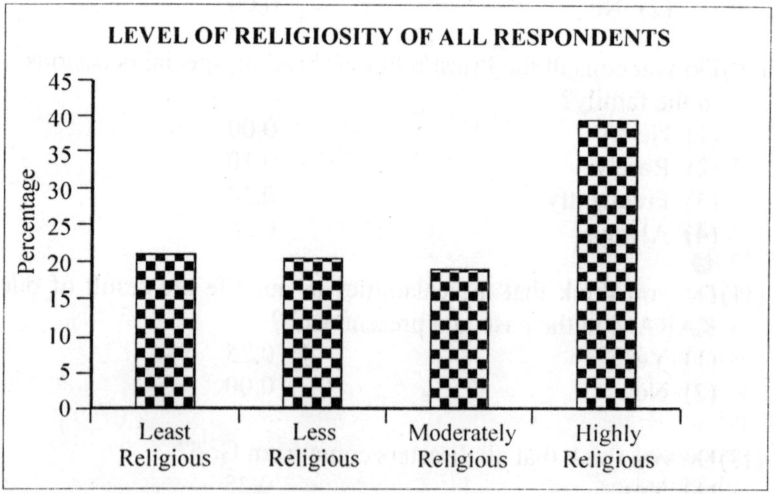

Fig. 5.7

than one-fifth of the respondents have come out to be the least religious, while almost the equal number has come out to be less religious. A closer look of the questionnaire shows that they have become less superstitions, lesser believer in the climates as the punishment of God and performing the special *pooja* at various occasions. Nearly 19 per cent of the total respondents have moderate belief in religion, while a little less than two-fifths have high belief in it.

The above analysis represents the aggregate picture of level of religiosity but there are a lot of inter and intra-caste and rural-urban variations in the level of religiosity. Table 5.16 which indicates the level of religiosity among the scheduled castes respondents shows that 256 scheduled caste respondents accounting to 23 per cent have strong belief in religion, while about 20 per cent are comparatively less religious (Fig.5.8). About 40 per cent respondents have reported to be highly religious, while 191 respondents amounting to 17 per cent have come out to

Table 5.16 : Level of Religiosity of All Scheduled Caste Respondents

Religious Group	*Score Range*	*No. of Respondents*	*%age to total*
Least Religious	<1.25	256	23.02
Less Religious	1.25-1.50	221	19.87
Moderately Religious	1.51-1.75	191	17.18
Highly Religious	>1.75	444	39.92
Total		**1112**	**100.00**

be moderately religious. The general inference from this also could be drawn that level of religiosity among scheduled caste respondents have gone down.

A closer look at the questionnaire and master table indicates variations in the level of religiosity among rural and urban scheduled caste respondents. Surprisingly, the rural scheduled castes have reported to be less religious as compared to urban scheduled castes. For example about 45 per cent of the rural scheduled caste is less religious, while the corresponding figure for urban scheduled castes is 37. About 39 per cent of the rural scheduled caste is highly religious as against 44 per cent of urban scheduled castes. This differential could be explained in terms of casual treatment of the rural respondents regarding the religion and also various restrictions imposed upon them for practicing religion.

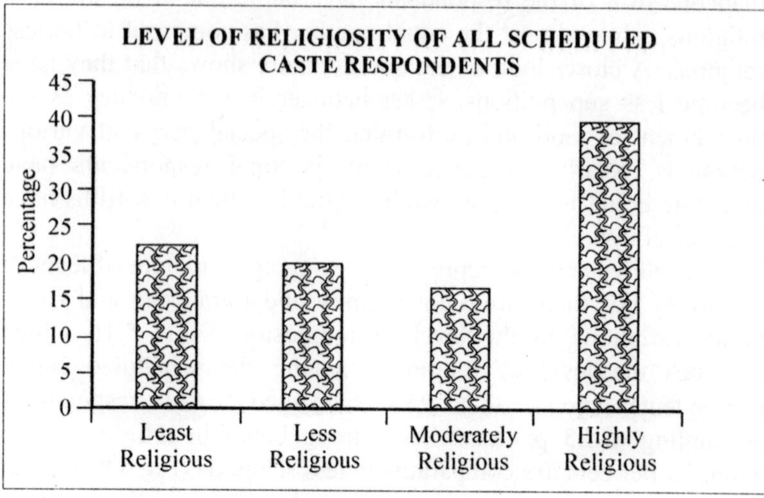

Fig. 5.8

Table 5.17 shows that the non-scheduled caste respondents, by and large, do not believe in superstitions, rituals, belief and religious performances. Hence, the level of religiosity has come down. Out of 398 non-scheduled caste respondents 17 per cent have preferred to be strongly religious, while around 23 per cent have come out to be less religious. As such about 44 per cent of

Table 5.17 : Level of Religiosity of All Non-Scheduled Caste Respondents

Religious Group	*Score Range*	*No. of Respondents*	*%age to total*
Least Religious	<1.25	63	15.83
Less Religious	1.25-1.50	91	22.86
Moderately Religious	1.51-1.75	93	23.37
Highly Religious	>1.75	151	37.94
Total		**398**	**100.00**

the total non-scheduled castes have turned out to be fewer believers in the religion. Nearly 38 per cent have gone into category of highly religious, while 23 belong to moderate category. This lower level of religiosity can be explained in terms of their more exposure to the urbanisation, mass media and higher level of education which eventually affect their religious belief.

Among the non-scheduled castes a lot of difference is found in the level of religiosity in rural and urban respondents. The urban non-scheduled castes, by and large, are more religious than their counterpart rural scheduled castes. Table 5.18 gives a comparative level of religiosity among all rural and urban respondents. It indicates that, by and large, the rural respondents are less religious as compared to the urban respondents. For example, nearly 42 per cent of the total rural respondents have come out to be less religious, while 38 per cent of the urban respondents belong to this category. Likewise about 44 per cent of the urban respondents are highly religious, while corresponding figure for rural respondents is 38. This rural-urban differential could be explained in terms of social and religious segregation of the scheduled castes in the rural areas. The rural poor especially the scheduled castes do not have

Table 5.18 : Level of Religiosity of All Rural and Urban Respondents

Religious Group	*Score Range*	*No. of Rural Respondents*	*% age to total*	*No. of Urban Respondents*	*%age to total*
Least Religious	<1.25	240	20.98	79	21.58
Less Religious	1.25-1.50	250	21.85	62	16.94
Moderately Religious	1.51-1.75	219	19.14	65	17.76
Highly Religious	>1.75	435	38.03	160	43.72
Total		**1144**	**100.00**	**366**	**100.00**

the access to many of the religious places nor they have direct approach to the religious priest. As such in case of many questions posed to assess the level of religiosity negative answers have been given by them.

Political Awareness and Involvement

The politics is so deeply interwoven in the fabrics of our daily life that no facet of it can remain in political isolation. The political behavior of Indian masses can no more be taken for granted but they have to be wooed, conversed and cajoled. They have gradually learnt the art of claiming their share of national cake. The democratic process involving different elections right from the Member of Parliament down to the *panchayat* elections has created awakening, interest and involvement among the rural masses. The scheduled castes who have a major consolidated vote bank have also become more conscious about their political rights and privileges. But their level of awakening is not uniform across the board. There are a number of factors which contribute to it. Therefore, an attempt has been made to assess the political awareness and involvement among the scheduled castes as well as non-scheduled castes by imposing a number of questions related to national and international political affairs. Queries were made regarding their involvement at national level and local level politics. Certain questions related to their political perceptions were also posed to the respondents. As the nature of the questions posed and the responses received were not of the similar nature and character, it was difficult to aggregate them. Therefore, the responses of the respondents were given weighted score as given here.

Scoring Scheme of Political Awareness and Involvement

(1) Do you know your :

(a) M.P.

(1) Yes	:	0.15
(2) No	:	0.00
(3) Name	:	0.25

(b) M.L.A.

(1) Yes	:	0.10
(2) No	:	0.00
(3) Name	:	0.20

(c) Chief Minister of U.P.

(1) Yes	:	0.15
(2) No	:	0.00
(3) Name	:	0.30

(d) V.L.W.

(1) Yes	:	0.10
(2) No	:	0.00
(3) Name	:	0.10

(e) Patwari

(1) Yes	:	0.10
(2) No	:	0.00
(3) Name	:	0.10

(2) Do you go to listen to political leader when he comes to your area?

(1) Always : 0.20
(2) Rarely : 0.15
(3) Never : 0.00

(3) Do you take active part in organizing such party meetings?

(1) Yes : 0.15
(2) No : 0.00

(4) Have you worked for any party in Assembly Election?

(1) Yes : 0.15
(2) No : 0.00
If yes,
(1) Manager : 0.15
(2) Agent : 0.05
(3) Convessor : 0.15
(4) Any other : 0.05

(5) Do you cast your vote at the time of election?

(1) Regularly : 0.15
(2) Rarely : 0.10
(3) Never : 0.00

(6) Have you visited the following while in session?

(a) Assembly
(1) Never : 0.00
(2) Rarely : 0.20
(3) Frequently : 0.40

(b) Parliament
(1) Never : 0.00
(2) Rarely : 0.20
(3) Frequently : 0.40

(7) Are you aware of P.M's Lahore Bus Journey?

(1) Yes : 0.20
(2) No : 0.00

respondents were arranged in ascending order of their score and grouped into three categories (Table 5.19). Table 5.19 showing the

Table 5.19 : Level of Political Awareness and Involvement of All Respondents

Category	*Score Range*	*No. of Respondents*	*%age to total*
Less Involved	<1.00	702	46.49
Moderately Involved	1.00-1.50	447	29.60
More Involved	>1.50	361	23.91
Total		**1510**	**100.00**

degree of political awareness and involvement of the selected respondents indicates that around 46 per cent of the respondents are poorly involved in the political affairs at national or international levels, whereas about 30 per cent fall under moderate category (Fig.5.9). The remaining around 24 per cent are highly involved in political affairs. This statistical analysis clearly indicates the higher involvement of the masses specially the scheduled castes into the national and local level politics.

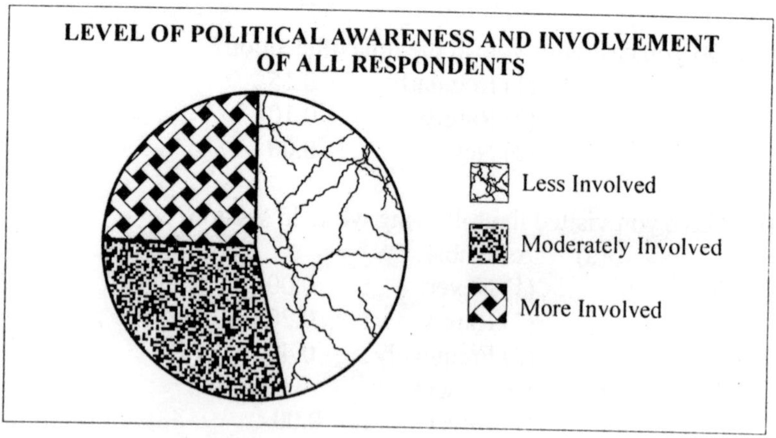

Fig. 5.9

The above analysis shows the aggregate picture of the political awareness and involvement of all the selected respondents but there are differences among the scheduled caste and non-scheduled caste respondents. Table 5.20 showing the political awareness and involvement of scheduled caste respondents indicates that 540 respondents out of 1112 scheduled caste respondents are poorly involved in political affairs, while 29 per cent are moderately involved (Fig.5.10).

Table 5.20 : Level of Political Awareness and Involvement of All Scheduled Caste Respondents

Category	*Score Range*	*No. of Respondents*	*%age to total*
Less Involved	<1.00	540	48.56
Moderately Involved	1.00-1.50	326	29.32
More Involved	>1.50	246	22.12
Total		**1112**	**100.00**

There are 246 respondents covering 22 per cent of the scheduled caste respondents are highly involved in political matters. These figures are clear indicator of the more and more involvement of the scheduled castes in the political affairs which is a positive sign of social transformation.

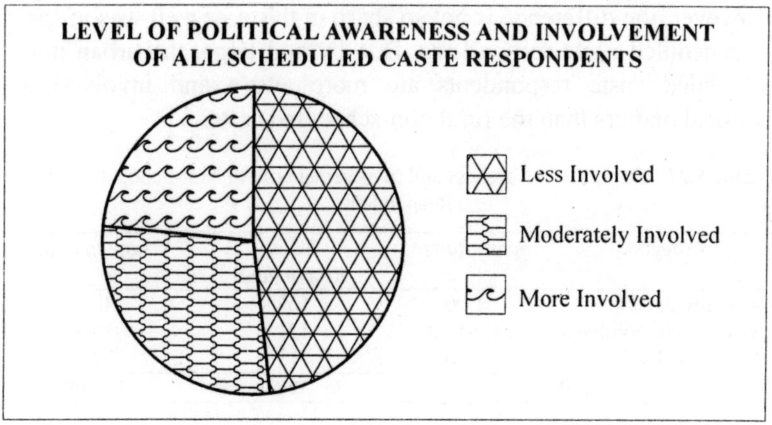

Fig. 5.10

There is much rural-urban differential among the scheduled caste respondents regarding political awareness and involvement. A cursory glance at the master table indicates that, by and large, the urban respondents have higher degree of political awareness and involvement as against the rural respondents. It has been found that about 33 per cent urban respondents are more involved in political affairs as against only 18 per cent in case of rural respondents.

involvement as against the rural respondents. It has been found that about 33 per cent urban respondents are more involved in political affairs as against only 18 per cent in case of rural respondents. Similarly, the percentage of less involved in political matters also varies. Nearly 43 per cent urban respondents fall under this category, while more than half of rural respondents fall in this group.

There is also perceptible difference in the political awareness and involvement between scheduled caste and non-scheduled caste respondents. By and large, the non-scheduled caste respondents are much more politically involved and aware of than the scheduled caste respondents. Table 5.21 indicates that about 29 per cent of non-scheduled caste respondents are more involved, while nearly 41 per cent are less involved. The corresponding figure for these two categories in case of scheduled caste respondents are 22 and 49 respectively. Among the non-scheduled caste respondents also there is difference in urban and rural non-scheduled caste respondents. However, the difference is not so sharp in this case as it was in case of scheduled caste respondents. But, by and large, the urban non-scheduled caste respondents are more aware and involved in political matters than the rural non-scheduled castes.

Table 5.21 : Degree of Awareness and Involvement of All Non-Scheduled Caste Respondents

Category	*Score Range*	*No. of Respondents*	*%age to total*
Less Involved	<1.00	162	40.70
Moderately Involved	1.00-1.50	121	30.40
More Involved	>1.50	115	28.90
Total		**398**	**100.00**

The aggregate picture of all urban and rural respondents with regard to political involvement and awareness is also inconformity with the all scheduled caste and non-scheduled caste respondents. A little less than one-third of the urban respondents are more involved in political affairs, while corresponding figure in case of all rural respondents is about 21 per cent. Likewise 43 per cent urban respondents are less involved in political affairs whereas 48 per cent rural respondents fall into this category. From the above discussion it may be concluded that there has been much political awareness and involvement of the masses in general and the scheduled castes in particular in the region. However, there is still much needs to be done to increase their level of political awareness and involvement.

Level of Social Mobility

Mobility is a process through which an individual is physically and mentally exposed to outside of his community and the world. Mobility, by and large, symbolises progressiveness. Mobility paves the path of progress, while immobility leads to stagnation. A mobile person gets exposed to a wide range of human endeavour. Repeated exposure to new ideas and increasing familiarity with new socio-cultural order speeds up the process of social change and provides impetus towards greater socio-economic transformation. The process and speed of mobility depends on mode of mobility which is the function of availability of transport infrastructure of the state on the one hand and the individual's capability to have his own means of transport on the other hand which is again the manifestation of economic importance. However, mobility is a powerful indicator of socio-economic transformation. Therefore, the mobility in general and social mobility in particular has been worked out with the help of well defined indicators such as visits to the friends and relations in the nearby areas and distant places, mode of transport — both public and private, the frequency of visit to various administrative headquarters and officials, market centres, fairs and exhibition and religious places. As the mode of transport, places and persons visited, distance travelled etc. are different, they have been given weighted score in order to bring them at uniform level. The mobility scores of all the respondents have been worked out separately, and finally, they have been classified into three categories on the basis of standard score of change. Table 5.22 indicates that about 18 per cent of the total respondents are highly

Table 5.22 : Level of Social Mobility of All Respondents

Category	*Score Range*	*No. of Respondents*	*%age to total*
Less Mobile	<1.50	991	65.63
Moderately Mobile	1.5.-1.75	244	16.16
More Mobile	>1.75	275	18.21
Total		**1510**	**100.00**

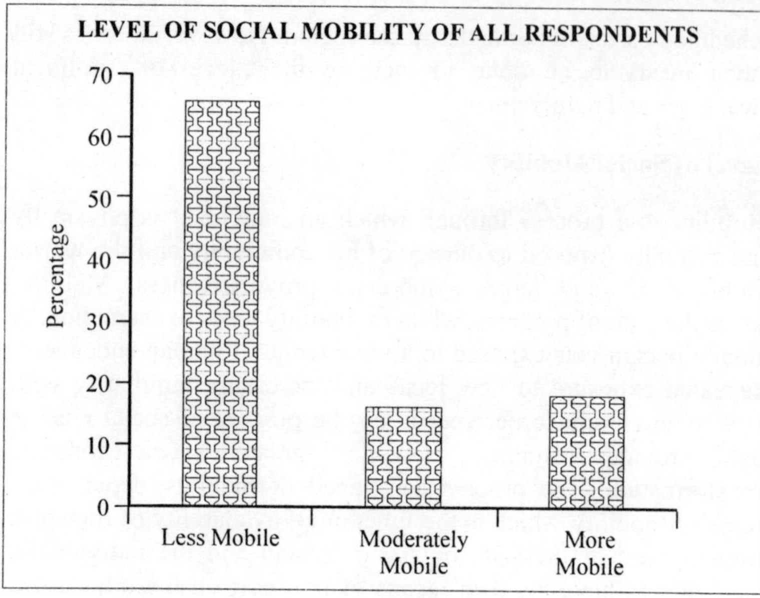

Fig. 5.11

mobile using their own conveyance and frequently visiting friends, relations and government officials. There are 244 respondents covering 16 per cent of the total respondents who are moderately mobile (Fig. 5.11). As such about one-third of the total respondents are more mobile which is an indicator of social transformation. Less than two-thirds of the respondents have come out to be less mobile because of their poor economic conditions and lesser contacts with the officials. As most of these respondents are either scheduled castes or belong to less income group, their level of education is also low. Hence, there are social inhibition and economic constraints in the process of their mobility.

Therefore, it is suggested that their educational level and economic conditions should be improved by giving various kind of incentives.

The above analysis indicates the aggregate status of the social mobility of the respondents but there are inter and intra-caste and residential differences in the level of social mobility. Table 5.23 shows that the scheduled caste respondents are comparatively less mobile as compared to the non-scheduled caste respondents. There are 187 scheduled caste respondents amounting to 16.8 per cent of the total who have come in the category of highly mobile, while 17 per cent fall in the moderate category (Fig. 5.12). The

Table 5.23 : Level of Social Mobility of All Scheduled Caste Respondents

Category	*Score Range*	*No. of Respondents*	*%age to total*
Less Mobile	<1.50	734	66.01
Moderately Mobile	1.50-1.75	191	17.17
More Mobile	>1.75	187	16.82
Total		**1112**	**100.00**

remaining two-thirds have been reported to be less mobile. This comparatively lower level of mobility among the scheduled caste as compare to the total respondents and non-scheduled caste respondents is due to their poor socio-economic conditions which needs overall upliftment. However, as compared to the past, they have definitely become mobile which is a sign of social transformation among the scheduled caste respondents.

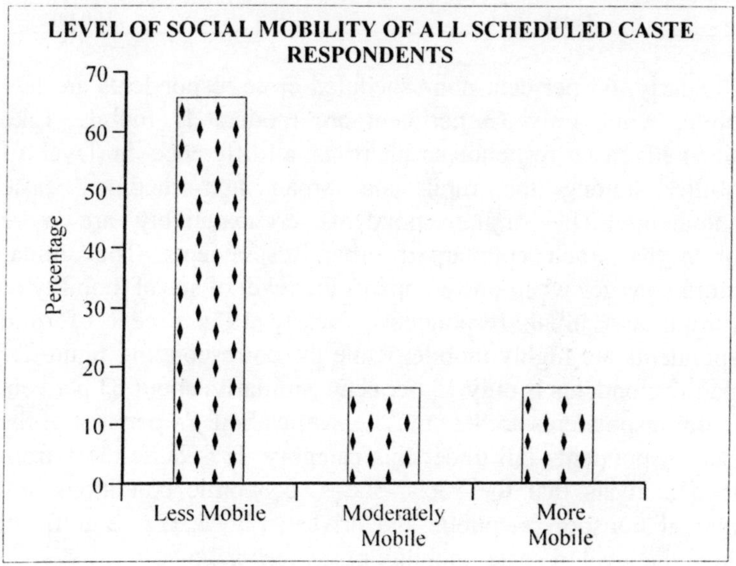

Fig. 5.12

Among the scheduled caste respondents there is a difference in social mobility among rural and urban respondents. By and large, rural respondents are more mobile than the urban ones which is simply because of the fact that the rural respondents have to cover longer distances to meet their relatives, friends and officials, whereas their counterpart, by and large, travel within the city. Further the rural respondents maintain better social relations with their relatives and friends by making frequent visits to their places, whereas it is lacking among the urban respondents. As pointed out earlier, the social mobility among the non-scheduled caste respondents is more as compare to scheduled caste respondents. There are 88 respondents out of 398 amounting to 22 per cent of the total who are highly mobile (Table 5.24). This high mobility score is because they have their own motor bike, jeep and car and they travel longer distances to maintain their social and official relations.

Table 5.24 : Level of Social Mobility of All Non-Scheduled Caste Respondents

Category	*Score Range*	*No. of Respondents*	*%age to total*
Less Mobile	<1.50	257	64.57
Moderately Mobile	1.5.-1.75	53	13.32
More Mobile	>1.75	88	22.11
Total		**398**	**100.00**

Nearly, 65 per cent non-scheduled caste respondents are less mobile, while only 13 per cent are moderately mobile. Like scheduled caste respondents there is a difference in level of mobility among the rural and urban non-scheduled caste respondents. The rural respondents comparatively are more mobile than their counterpart urban respondents. The similar picture emerges when one compares the level of social mobility of all rural and urban respondents. Nearly 19 per cent of rural respondents are highly mobile, while the corresponding figure for urban respondents is only 15 per cent. Similarly, about 63 per cent of rural respondents are less mobile, while about 74 per cent of the urban respondents fall under this category. It is quite clear from above analysis that the social status, economic conditions and mode of transport — public and private, play a very significant role in the level of social mobility of the respondents.

Overall Level of Social Transformation

In the preceding discussion the social transformation has been described and explained with respect to 6 selected indicators which have shown positive and encouraging level of change at differential levels. As these indicators are of different nature and character and have been given different scoring scheme, they can not be directly averaged out in order to get overall level of social transformation. Therefore, a composite Index of social transformation with the help of the following formula has been worked out :

$$\text{Composite Index of Transformation (CIT)} = \frac{\sum_{i=1}^{N} Xij}{N}$$

Where, Xij = score value of ith social element
N = number of social elements

The result thus obtained is 3.10 in which 0.40 is added and a rounded scale of more than 3.50 scores (High), 3.50-2.50 scores (Medium) and less than 2.50 scores (Low) has been taken to classify the respondents. Consequently the respondents have been grouped into three categories based on their individual scores of social transformation (Table 5.25).

Table 5.25 : Composite Index of Social Transformation

Category	*Score Range*	*No. of Respondents*	*%age of Total*
High	> 3.50	286	25.56
Medium	3.50-2.50	498	32.98
Low	< 2.50	626	41.46
Total		**1510**	**100.00**

Table 5.25 gives very encouraging result of social transformation indicating that about one-fourth of the total respondents have high level of social transformation, while almost one-third fall in the medium category. The scrutiny of individual score of transformation of respondents indicates that about half of respondents have scores higher than the standard scale of social transformation and the substantial number of them belong to non-scheduled caste respondents with agricultural land. However, a little more than two-fifths of respondents have low level of transformation and majority of them belong to scheduled castes.

REFERENCES

Dreze, J. and Kingdon, G., 2001: School Participation in Rural India *Review of Development Economics*, 5.

Everett, J.M.,1981: *Women and Social Change in India*, Heritage Pub., Delhi.

Farro, T.J., 2001: *Social Action System and Synthesis in Sociological Theory,* Preger, Westport.

Gore, M. S., 1985: *Social Aspect of Development*, Rawat Pub., Jaipur.

Joshi, P.C., 1989: *Culture, Communication and Social Change*, Vikas Pub., New Delhi.

Kabilan, R., 1993: *From Traditional Society to Post Industrial Society*, Common Wealth Pub., New Delhi.

Kingdon, G., 1996: 'The Quality and Efficiency of Private and Public Education: A Case Study of Urban India', *Oxford Bulletin of Economics and Statistics*, 58(1), 57-82.

Mohammad, N., 1992: Spatial Variations in Levels of Development in U.P. in Mohammad, N., (ed.) *New Dimensions in Agricultural Development*, Concept Pub. Co., New Delhi.

Nartu, P., 2001: *Dynamics of Social Structure and Change*, Dnam. Co. Pub. Delhi.

Pasachropoulos, G., 1988: 'Education and Development: A Review', *World Bank Research Observer,* 3(1), 99-116.

Pathak, *Continuity and Change in Indian Society*, Concept Pub. Co., New Delhi.

Raychaudhuri, S.P. and Others, 1963 : *Soils of India,* New Delhi.

Roy Burman, B.K., 1994: *Tribes in Perspective*, Mittal Publications, Delhi.

Sathyamurthy, T.V., *Class Transformation and Practical Transformation in Post Colonial India*, New Delhi.

Singh, J., 1984: *Agricultural Geography*, Tata McGrow-Hill Pub. Co., New Delhi.

Stern, R.W., 1993: *Changing India*, Cambridge University Press, New Delhi.

Vajpaeyi, K., 1979: *Modernisation and Social Change in India*, Manohar Pub., New Delhi.

Zhianska, L. and Dinitrova, M., 1986: *Society and Social Change*, Svyat Pub., Safia.

6

LEVEL OF ECONOMIC TRANSFORMATION

Ever since independence government has formulated and implemented various programmes and policies for the overall development of the country. Many of these programmes had been directly related with the upliftment of the rural masses in general and scheduled castes in particular. The aggregate effect of all these programmes and policies is manifested in overall economic prosperity of the rural masses. Many of them have got agricultural land by the government under different schemes of land distribution and have started agricultural practices. A considerable segment of scheduled castes are now working in non-agricultural sectors like building construction, factories and in private shops in urban centres within and outside the area. The educated rural scheduled castes prefer non-agricultural activities and a considerable number of such youths are in marketing, educational, administrative and judicial services. Some of them have established their own commercial and industrial enterprises under the self-employment scheme of the government. All these have helped in increasing their level of income which has brought economic transformation.

For the economic transformation there could be several indicators but it is very difficult to generate data for all these indicators. Therefore, for the assessment of economic transformation income level, standard of living, housing condition, exposure to mass media and level of occupational diversification have been taken into consideration. A brief account of each of these is given here. Besides these, land holding size, patterns of landuse in kharif and rabi seasons, and level of innovativeness have already been discussed in Chapter Fourth accounting the socio-economic structure of the respondents.

Level of Per Capita Income

After independence India has been persistently trying to increase the per capita income so as to raise the standard of living of its masses by inducting various programmes and policies during different Five Year Plans which have actually started bearing the fruit after mid-sixties when the Green Revolution Programme was launched. Subsequently various other programmes of rural upliftment especially for weaker and downtrodden section of the society were introduced which have diversified the occupational structure of the rural masses and subsequently have helped in increasing their income level. They have switched over to more remunerative occupations. Consequently per capita income of scheduled caste population has also increased. Although per capita income is very good indicator for the assessment of economic status, but the collection of data especially in rural set-up of diversified occupational structure with no fixed income or daily wages is a Herculean task. It is more so when there is no system of maintaining the record of the income. However, in order to work out per capita income of the respondents, the earnings of all family members in whatsoever form it was, were ascertained by putting several questions in different forms. The total earnings including agricultural produce of the household, thus ascertained, was converted into monetary value with a uniform standard conversion scale, and finally, divided with the total members of the household. The results thus obtained gives per capita income of the family member which has been compared with their earlier calculated per capita income for a decade before. Subsequently, weighted scores have been given and level of change is ascertained. Finally, based on the results, the respondents have been grouped into three categories (Table 6.1).

Table 6.1 : Index of Income Level

Category	*Income Range*	*No. of Respondent*	*%age of total*
Low	< 1,000	609	40.33
Medium	1,000-2,000	574	38.01
High	> 2,000	327	21.6
Total		**1510**	**100.00**

Table 6.1 shows that around two-fifths of the total respondents fall under low-income group, while about 38 per cent fall under medium category. As such nearly 78 per cent respondents do not have enough income to maintain a reasonable standard of living. A closer look at the master table indicates that majority of these respondents belong to scheduled caste population. About 22 per cent respondents belong to higher income group. Many of them are non-scheduled caste respondents with large size of holdings.

Level of Standard of Living

In fact the standard of living is a very effective indicator to gauge the socio-economic condition of the people. Although mere observation and making qualitative comments of standard of living is easier but its quantitative measurement is comparatively difficult because it is, by and large, manifestation of income, housing condition, dress and dressing materials, household utensils, exposure to mass media, social status and a host of such conditions. Per capita income is, perhaps, the main factor but it is not everything for the assessment of standard of living. However, in order to gauge it, various pin pointed and inferential questions were framed and administered on various possible parameters considered to be contributing to standard of living. As the nature of quaries and the responses of the respondents were of varied nature, judicious scores have been given to them, and on this basis the standard of living and the changes therein have been worked out for all the respondents who have been classified into three categories according to the scale of standard score of change (Table 6.2).

Table 6.2 : Level of Standard of Living

Category	*Score Range*	*No. of Respondent*	*%age to total*
Low	<2.5	686	45.43
Medium	2.5-3.5	529	35.03
High	>3.5	295	19.54
Total		**1510**	**100.00**

The above analysis and observation of the collected facts and semi-processed data reveal many obvious results about the degree of change in standard of living of the scheduled castes. Their income level and housing conditions have considerably improved. They have diversified their occupations adopting more remunerative ones so as to increase their income level. Higher level of exposure to mass media is also a surrogate indicator of high standard of living. Earlier they had hardly footwear, and even if they had, they use to wear it only on ceremonial occasions but now almost every men and women wear at least *chappal,* if not shoes, and better quality shoes on ceremonial occasions. They are comparatively better dressed specially the educated ones who wear pant and colourful shirts. Their food habits and quality of food have also improved. They no longer rely on parched grain with piece of *gur* or salt and a jug of water as breakfast or with two breads with salt and onion as their lunch. The social status has also improved mainly due to their vote bank which now a days is not blindly utilized, and partly due to their improved economic condition and overall awareness among them. As a result of all these a little less than one-fifth of the total respondents fall in the high category. A close look at the master table indicates that most of these respondents are non-scheduled caste respondents with larger size of land holdings. Nearly 35 per cent respondents come under medium category. It includes the creamy layer of the scheduled castes and almost all the remaining non-scheduled caste respondents. About 45 per cent respondents have lower standard of living. Majority of these are scheduled castes.

Level of Housing Condition

The house is an individuals identity symbol reflecting ones socio-economic status and prestige. A suitable house is one of those basic needs of human life without which one cannot conceive of a life worth living. It influences ones physical health and mental efficiency. Consequently it affects the skill and productivity which ultimately determines individuals socio-economic status. Prior to independence or even up to two decades later, the houses of the rural masses in general and scheduled castes in particular were in bad shape and were mainly made of mud walls and thatched roofs which they could not renovate annually due to lack of financial resources. They use to keep their cows, goats, pigs and other animals, if at all they were there, in one of the corners of the same house. But as the process of development has brought economic prosperity even scheduled castes have started investing a lot in improving their housing condition. They are gradually changing their mud-thatched houses into mud-tiles, brick-tiles and ultimately into reinforced bricks and cement *(RBC)* houses. Reinforced cement and concrete (RCC) houses are also frequently observed.

Housing is a universally complex commodity and it is difficult to gauge and compare them in totality. Even if they look the same, they are infinitely varied in character and quality, and whatever single measure is adopted, none by itself appears to reflect all variations attributed to house size, location, architectural style, various infrastructural facilities etc. It is even more complex in rural areas. With this view as many as 16 questions related to various component of houses such as size, location, architectural style, storage, number of rooms, courtyard, guestroom, building material, household utensils, toilet, arrangement for livestocks etc. have been taken into account in this study. Since the attributes of the house are varied and complex and the response of the respondents were also varied and different, it was not possible to make comparative assessment of the status of their housing condition. Hence, judicious scores have been given to responses of the respondents to various attributes of houses. Finally, the scores of the individual respondents with respect to housing condition have been added in order to get there housing score. Based on the housing scores, the respondents have been grouped into three categories (Table 6.3).

Table 6.3 : Housing Condition of All Respondents

Category	*Score Range*	*No. of Respondents*	*%age to total*
Poor	<4.50	438	29.01
Moderate	4.50-6.00	744	49.27
Good	>6.00	328	21.72
Total		**1510**	**100.00**

Table 6.3 shows that the houses of around 22 per cent of the total respondents are good, while a little less than 50 per cent come under moderate category. Nearly 29 per cent of respondents have poor housing conditions (Fig. 6.1). This statistical account clearly shows that the overall housing condition of the rural masses in India has improved. It is also true in case of the scheduled caste respondents who were earlier living in one room along with their all belongings including the cattle.

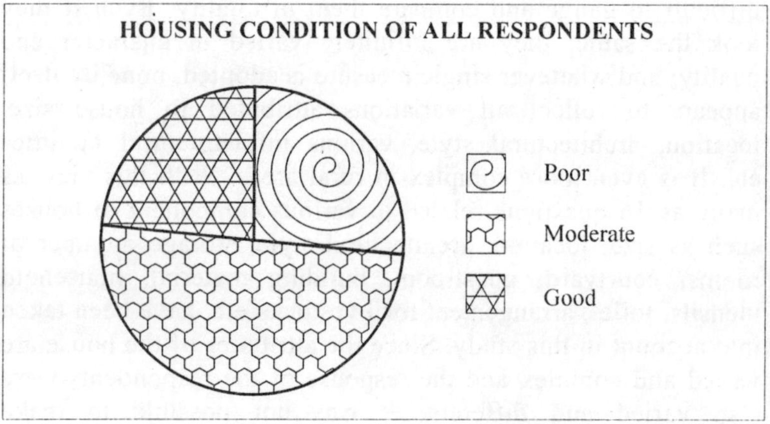

Fig. 6.1

Table 6.4 shows the status of the house of the scheduled caste respondents which indicates that almost one-third of scheduled caste respondents have poor housing facilities, while nearly 52 per cent belong to the moderate category. Out of the 1112 scheduled caste respondents, 172 amounting to around 15

Table 6.4 : Housing Condition of All Scheduled Caste Respondents

Category	*Score Range*	*No. of Respondents*	*%age to total*
Poor	< 4.50	362	32.55
Moderate	4.50-6.00	578	51.98
Good	> 6.00	172	15.47
Total		**1112**	**100.00**

per cent of the total have better housing facilities (Fig.6.2). These statistical figures and the cursory glance at the questionnaire and the master table clearly show much improvement in the housing condition of scheduled castes which is a sign of economic transformation.

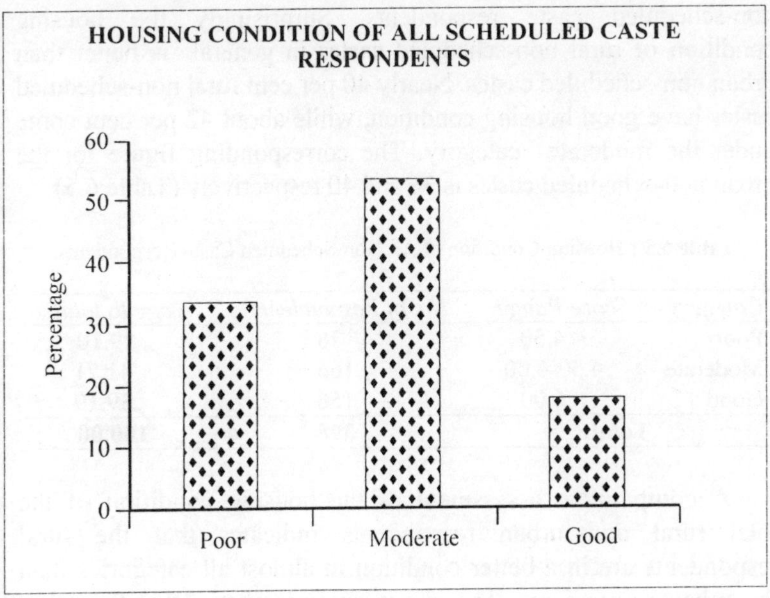

Fig. 6.2

A comparative view of the rural and the urban scheduled caste respondents does not show much difference in the housing condition of both the categories. This is, perhaps, due to the fact that even the urban scheduled castes do not have the better housing condition than the non-scheduled castes in the urban centres.

It is interesting to note that the housing conditions of the non-scheduled caste respondents are far better than the scheduled caste respondents. Out of 398 non-scheduled caste respondents, 156 amounting to about 39 per cent of the total have good houses, while around 42 per cent have the moderate category of houses. The corresponding figures for the scheduled caste respondents for these categories are 15 and 52 respectively. Only 19 per cent of non-scheduled castes have poor housing conditions. It may be inferred from the above analysis that non-scheduled caste respondents are economically better of than scheduled caste respondents and there level of economic transformation is higher than their counterpart.

There is rural–urban differential in the housing condition of non-scheduled caste respondents. Surprisingly the housing condition of rural non-scheduled castes in general is better than urban non-scheduled castes. Nearly 40 per cent rural non-scheduled castes have good housing condition, while about 42 per cent come under the moderate category. The corresponding figure for the urban non-scheduled castes is 36 and 40 respectively (Table 6.5).

Table 6.5 : Housing Condition of All Non-Scheduled Caste Respondents

Category	*Score Range*	*No. of Respondents*	*%age to total*
Poor	< 4.50	76	19.10
Moderate	4.50-6.00	166	41.71
Good	> 6.00	156	39.19
Total		**398**	**100.00**

A comparative assessment of the housing condition of the total rural and urban respondents indicates that the rural respondents are in a better condition in almost all categories than the urban respondents. The above analysis shows that there has been overall improvement in the housing condition of the respondents, which is an indicator of economic transformation.

Level of Exposure to Mass Media

Exposure to mass media is an irrefutable indicator of socio-economic transformation as it reaches the audience more easily and many a times directly, and affects knowledge, attitude, opinion and behaviour of individual. It not only exposes the masses regarding various innovations and technologies in different fields but it also demonstrates the benefits and achievements of people who have opted them. With this backlog an attempt has been made to assess the level of exposure of the respondents by posing questions regarding various sources of mass media such as radio, transistor, television, newspaper, magazine, fair, exhibition, motion pictures etc. Queries were also made regarding their participation and involvement in them. As the questions and the responses in this connection were of different nature and character, weighted scores are allotted to different components in order to facilitate the comparability of data and its subsequent quantification. The total scores of the individuals have been worked out and they have been grouped into three categories. The resulting figures are given in Table 6.6.

Table 6.6 : Level of Exposure to Mass Media of All Respondents

Category	*Score Range*	*No. of Respondents*	*%age to total*
Less Exposed	< 2.0	174	13.07
Moderately Exposed	2.0-5.0	553	41.55
More Exposed	> 5.0	604	45.38
Total		**1331**	**100.00**

A glance at individual score shows that there is a lot of variation in its ranging from 1.00 to 7.5 scores. But larger number of respondents are on the higher side. Table 6.6 showing the level of exposure of respondents to mass media indicates that nearly 45 per cent respondents are highly exposed to mass media, while about 42 per cent are moderately exposed. The higher level of exposure is due to the fact that radio and transistors have become very common, and television is gaining popularity. The increasing level of literacy, the newspapers and magazines, specially the local ones, are also contributing to the level of exposure. Moreover, tea stalls, *chaupals,* market places and many such other places of gathering are also contributing a lot to the level of exposure because here people not only discuss the political affairs of local, national and international nature but many innovative technologies and their achievements are also discussed which ultimately enhance their level of exposure.

The level of exposure to mass media of scheduled caste respondents has been given in Table 6.7 which shows that their level of exposure is almost in conformity with all the respondents with slight variations, i.e. in the higher category there are 42 per cent respondents, while it is 45 per cent in case of all respondents. Likewise, in the moderate category 45 per cent scheduled caste respondents are covered, while it is 42 per cent in case of all respondents (Fig.6.3). This is because of the fact that the transistor, radio and other mass media have been common, and are becoming more common among the scheduled caste respondents also. This statistical account leads us to draw a fair conclusion of higher level of exposure of scheduled caste respondents to mass media.

Table 6.7 : Level of Exposure to Mass Media of All Scheduled Caste Respondents

Category	*Score Range*	*No. of Respondents*	*%age to total*
Less Exposed	< 2.0	133	13.68
Moderately Exposed	2.0-5.0	435	44.75
More Exposed	> 5.0	404	41.57
Total		972	100.00

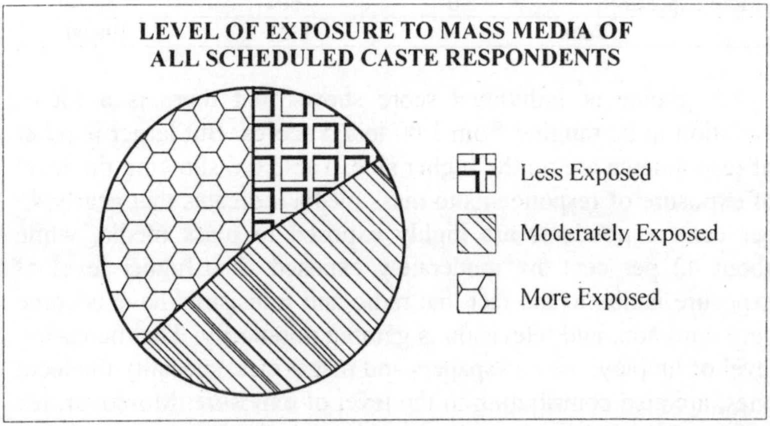

Fig. 6.3

A closer look at the questionnaire and the master table shows that the urban scheduled caste respondents are much more exposed to the mass media than their counterpart rural scheduled castes. This is because of the fact that urban scheduled castes are more educated, have better infrastructural facilities and have more access to various mass media. However, nearly 58 per cent of the urban scheduled castes are highly exposed, while about 32 per cent are moderately exposed. Both the categories added together account nine-tenths of the total scheduled caste respondents leaving only 10 per cent who are less exposed.

The level of exposure of non-scheduled caste respondents to mass media is even better than the all respondents and scheduled caste respondents. They are more exposed to mass media. Table 6.8 showing the level of exposure to non-scheduled caste respondents to mass media shows that out of 359, 200 respondents amounting to about 56 per cent are highly exposed to mass media, while about one-third belong to moderate category. The remaining 11 per cent are less exposed. This high level of exposure of non-scheduled caste respondents can be explained in terms of their better economic condition resulting to have more instruments of mass media and the high level of education. But there are rural-

Table 6.8 : Level of Exposure to Mass Media of All Non-Scheduled Caste Respondents

Category	*Score Range*	*No. of Respondents*	*%age to total*
Less Exposed	<2.0	41	11.42
Moderately Exposed	2.0-5.0	118	32.87
More Exposed	>5.0	200	55.71
Total		**359**	**100.00**

urban differentials among the non-scheduled caste respondents also. As is expected the urban respondents are more exposed than the rural. There are about 64 per cent urban respondents who are highly exposed and nearly 35 per cent respondents are moderately exposed. The corresponding figures for both these categories in case of rural non-scheduled caste respondents are 54 and 32. Interestingly less than 2 per cent of urban respondents are less exposed to mass media. At the aggregate level also there is rural-urban differential in the level of exposure to mass media among the selected respondents. As expected the urban respondents are more exposed and 33 per cent are moderately exposed leaving only 8 per cent to less exposed respondents. The corresponding figure for the rural respondents are 41, 44 and 15 per cent respectively.

Level of Occupational Diversification

Due to induction of various programmes and policies by the government during the Five Year Plans and the growing awareness and awakening, the occupational structure of the masses has undergone a change. They are no longer satisfied with a single occupation and adopt various subsidiary occupations not only to meet the requirements of their household but also to increase their socio-economic status. A detailed account of it has already been given in Chapter Four dealing with socio-economic structure of the respondents. The study reveals that apart from agriculture which is the main occupation of 514 respondents, dairy farming, piggeries, fishing, poultry farming and labour are the other occupations which have been adopted by the respondents on commercial as well as subsistence basis. Out of 538 respondents 473 (87.0%) have adopted all these occupation on commercial basis, while 65 respondents (12%) on subsistence basis. All these respondents who have adopted it on commercial basis, do not consider it their main source of income. Only 110 (35%) respondents have treated it as their main income, while 203 (65%) practice it for subsidiary income. As all these occupations are of different nature, they cannot be aggregated. Hence, the weightage have been given in order to assess the occupational transformation and the results are represented in the Table 6.9.

Table 6.9 : Level of Occupational Transformation

Category	*Score Range*	*No. of Respondent*	*%age of total*
Low	< 2.00	190	35.32
Medium	2.0-3.0	211	39.22
High	> 3.0	137	25.46
	Total	**538**	**100.00**

Table 6.9 shows that a little more than one-fourth respondents have high level of change, while 211 respondents accounting nearly two-fifths of the total belong to medium category. The remaining 35 per cent fall in the low category. A closer look at the questionnaire and master-table indicates that there is not much difference in the occupational transformation either at inter-caste level or rural-urban level. By and large, younger generation and

educated respondents belong to higher category, while older ones and less educated fall either in medium or low category.

Overall Level of Economic Transformation

The above discussion and analysis of level of economic transformation with respect to selected economic indicators show inter and inter indicator variations in all of them. Hence, in order to get the aggregate picture of level of economic transformation the composite index of economic transformation has been worked out using the same formula used in overall social transformation.

The result obtained in this equation is 3.29 which has been rounded up to 3.50 and finally, three grades, viz. more than 3.50 scores, 3.50 to 2.50 and less than 2.50 scores have been identified. Accordingly the respondents have been grouped into three categories (Table 6.10).

Table 6.10 shows that about 16 per cent of the total respondents have recorded high economic transformation. A closer scrutiny of the master table shows that larger number of respondents under this category are non-scheduled caste respondents who comparatively have larger size of holding. About

Table 6.10 : Composite Index of Economic Transformation

Category	*Score Range*	*No. of Respondent*	*%age of total*
High	> 3.50	243	16.09
Medium	3.50-2.50	484	32.05
Low	< 2.50	783	51.86
Total		**1510**	**100.00**

32 per cent respondents have shown moderate change and they are distributed across all the categories of respondents. More than half of the respondents have shown low level of transformation and they are mostly poor respondents.

Level of Socio-Economic Transformation

Although while discussing and explaining various demographic characteristics such as age composition, educational status of respondents and household, attitude towards education, size of family, attitude towards family welfare programme, relegiosity, occupational structure and its transformation, housing condition, income level, standard of living, social mobility etc, the levels of social and economic transformation have been discussed at various level. However, in order to evaluate socio-economic transformation with reference to certain parameters, the composite index of socio-economic transformation has been worked out by using very simple technique with reference to rural-urban, educated and illiterate, young and old, economically well of and poor, and scheduled caste and non-scheduled caste respondents. The weighted scores of all parameters of change of the individuals of a category have been added together and divided by number of individuals in the category.

The result of this exercise reveals that the composite index of socio-economic transformation of the non-scheduled castes who account 26 per cent of the total respondents is 3.25, while in case of scheduled caste respondents who cover 76 per cent of the total is 2.19 (Table 6.11). It proves our first hypotheses i.e., *the level and rate of socio-economic transformation is more among the non-scheduled castes as compared to scheduled castes population.*

Table 6.11 : Composite Index of Socio-Economic Transformation of Respondents

S.No	*Types of Respondents*	*No. of Respondents*	*C. I. of Transformation*
1	Scheduled caste Respondents	1112	**2.19**
	Non-scheduled caste Respondents	398	**.3.25**
2	Younger Respondents (All)	607	**3.18**
	Older Respondents (All)	903	**1.63**
3	Economically well of Respondents	385	**3.84**
	Poor Respondents	1125	**1.97**
4	Urban scheduled castes	299	**2.95**
	Rural scheduled castes	813	**1.59**
5	Educated scheduled castes	485	**4.01**
	Illiterate scheduled castes	627	**1.39**

Table 6.11 also shows that the younger generation accounting 40 per cent of the total respondents have also high level of socio-economic transformation. The composite index in case of younger people is 3.18, whereas it is only 1.63 for older people. Hence, it may safely be inferred that *the level and rate of socio-economic transformation is more among the younger generation than the older ones,* which is our second hypotheses.

An attempt has also been made to work out the composite index of socio-economic transformation of economically well of and poor respondents who account 25 per cent and 75 per cent of the total respondents respectively. The composite index of the former is 3.84, while it is 1.97 in case of the latter. Hence, it proves our third hypotheses, viz. *the level and rate of socio-economic transformation is more among the economically well of scheduled castes as compared to poor ones.*

It has also been found that there are variations among the scheduled caste respondents in the level of socio-economic transformation. The urban scheduled caste respondents who account nearly 26 per cent of the total respondents have a composite index of 2.95 as against their rural counter part who have a composite index of 1.59, which also proves our fourth hypotheses, viz. *the level and rate of socio-economic transformation is more among the urban scheduled castes as against their rural counterpart*, although the difference among the two is not very high. Hence, it may be taken as the weaker link between the two.

Another difference in the level of socio-economic transformation among the scheduled caste population is found at the differential level of education. The results show that the educated scheduled castes which account 32 per cent of the total scheduled caste population have a composite index of 4.01, while corresponding figure is 1.39 in case of illiterate scheduled castes. This is a very heartening result showing considerable difference among the educated and non-educated scheduled castes. It also proves our fifth hypotheses which run as *the level and rate of socio-economic transformation is more among the educated scheduled castes as compared to illiterate scheduled castes.*

Overall Level of Socio-Economic Transformation

In the preceding analysis it has been found that there is a lot of variation in the levels of transformation not only in various selected socio-economic indicators but also in the aggregate of social and economic transformation. Therefore, in order to assess the overall socio-economic transformation a Composite Index of Transformation has been worked out using the following formula.

$$\text{Composite Index of Transformation (CIT)} = \frac{\sum_{i=1}^{N} Xij}{N}$$

Where, Xij = score value of ith element of socio-economic change
N = number of element of socio-economic change

The result obtained in this equation is 3.26 which have been rounded to 3.50. Taking one as an interval three categories, viz. High, Medium and Low have been formed and the respondents have been put in different categories as per their scores (Table 6.12).

Table 6.12 : Overall Level of Socio-Economic Transformation

Category	*Score Range*	*No. of Respondent*	*%age of total*
High	> 3.50	247	16.36
Medium	3.50-2.50	423	28.01
Low	< 2.50	840	55.63
Total		**1510**	**100.00**

Table 6.12 shows that around 16 per cent respondents have overall high level of socio-economic transformation. As has been pointed out earlier most of these respondents are non-scheduled caste respondents with reasonable size of land holding. Nearly 28 per cent respondents belong to medium level, while around 56 per cent have fallen in the low category. Most of them are either poor respondents or scheduled castes.

The major conclusions which could be derived from the above discussion and analysis are: *firstly,* there are considerable changes in all the socio-economic indicators chosen in this study; *secondly,* the level of change is not uniform in all the cases but there are inter and intra-indicator variations in both social and economic conditions; *thirdly*, there is higher level of transformation in economic conditions than that of social conditions which is in conformity with the general principle, viz. economic prosperity brings social transformation; and *fourthly,* the Composite Index of Transformation also shows high level of transformation. And, all these. points prove the proposed hypotheses. There are definitely strong positive changes which are bringing overall improvements in the condition of scheduled castes. Therefore, it is suggested that more and more facilities, incentives, loans and subsidies for various development and welfare programmes should be provided to scheduled castes so that their pace of progress increases and they could come up at par with the other castes and communities of the nation but without any kind of confrontation with them.

REFERENCES

Alexander, J.C.,1990: *Culture and Society: Contemporary Debate*, Cambridge University Press, Cambridge.

Asia Development Bank, 2001: *Growth and Change in Asia and the Pacific, (Key Indicators)*, Oxford University Press, Oxford.

Chakravarti, A., 2001: *Social Power and Everyday Class Relations : Agrarian Transformation in North Bihar.*

Chopra, K. and Gulati, S.C., 2001: *Migration, Common Property Resources and Environmental Degradation: Interlinkages in India's Arid and Semi-arid Regions,* Institute of Economic Growth, Delhi.

Hanumantha Rao, C.H. and Linneman, H.(eds.),1996: Economic Reforms and Poverty Alleviation in India: *Indo-Dutch Studies on Development Alternatives*,Vol.17.

Hayami, R. and Ruttan,V., 1971: *Agricultural Development: An International Perspective*, Johns Hopkins Press, Baltimore.

Hoda, A., 2002: 'WTO Agreement on Agriculture in India', in Hoda, A.(ed.), *WTO Agreement and Indian Agriculture,* Social Science Press, Delhi.

Kahkonen, S. and Olson, M. (eds.), 2001: *A New Institutional Approach to Economic Development.*

Krishanji, N. and Krishnan, T.N. (eds.) 2000: Public Support for Food Security: The Public Distribution System in India. *Strategies for Human Development in India*, Vol.1.

Kuznets, S.,1973: 'Modern Economic Growth: Findings and Reflections', *American Economic Review*, 13(3).

McGranahan, D., Pizarro, E. and Richard, C., 1985: *Measurement And Analysis of Socio-Economic Development*, N.N. Research Institute, Geneva.

Prabhu Seeta, K., 2001: *Economic Reform and Social Sector Development : A Study of Two Indian States*, UNDP India Country Office, New Delhi.

Prakash, B.A. (ed.),1999: *Kerala's Economic Development: Issues and Problems*, University of Kerala, Thiruvananthapuram.

Reynolds, L., 1983: 'Innovations and Adjustments in Economic Growth', *Swedish Journal of Economics*, 74(4).

Rogaly, B. and Barbara Harriss-White, Bose, S. (eds), 1999: *Sonar Bangla?* Agricultural Growth and Agrarian Change in West Bengal and Bangladesh.

Shiva, V. and Bedi, G. (eds.), 2002: *Sustainable Agriculture and Food Security : The Impact of Globalisation.*

Sundaram, K., and Tendulkar, S.D., 1988: *'Measurement of Poverty: Some Conceptual Problems'*, Paper No.36, Second Seminar on Social Statistics, Feb. 4-6, 1988, Central Statistical Organisation, New Delhi.

Tendulkar, S.D., 1992: 'Economic Growth and Poverty' in Hariss, B., Guhan, S. and Csssen, R.(eds) *Poverty in India: Research and Policy*, Oxford University Press, Bombay.

The World Bank,1990: *World Development Indicator*, Washington D.C.

Tornquist, O., 1999: *Politics and Development: A Critical Introduction,* Uppsala University.

World Bank, 1997: *World Development Report 1997*,Washington D.C.

7

CONCLUSION AND SUGGESTSIONS

The present study of socio-economic transformation of scheduled castes conducted in the erstwhile state of Uttar Pradesh which accounts about 21.17 per cent of the scheduled castes population of the country gives very interesting and heartening results. Although the total scheduled castes population in the state is 2,92,76,455, which amounts 21.05 per cent of the total population of the state, there are a lot of inter and intra-district variations in its spatial distributional pattern. However, on the basis of the percentage strength of scheduled castes population, the state has been divided into four regions, i.e. the region of high, moderate, low and very low concentrations. The region of high concentration is mainly confined in two blocks, viz. eastern districts of Uttrakhand and central U.P. Besides these, smaller pockets are also found in extreme east and southeastern parts of the state. Likewise the districts with moderate concentration are mainly found into two pockets, viz. eastern, central and western central parts of state. The distributional pattern of the low and very low categories of districts is even more uneven and scattered. However, in the present study 40 villages and 10 towns/cities have been selected from these regions. From these 50 settlement sites 1112 scheduled caste respondents and 398 non-scheduled caste respondents have been taken for in-depth study of socio-economic transformation and also inter and intra-caste variations in it.

Age composition of the population is very important parameter in the process of overall development in general and rural development in particular because it not only ascertains the workforce and level of dependency but a favourable age composition is also instrumental in the adoption of new ideas and practices which bring economic benefits and prosperity. Hence, if the leadership of household is in the hands of energetic younger generation, the probability of prosperity and overall change is more.

The study reveals that the younger generation of less than 30 years of age are coming forward in the decision making process of the household matters specially related with the economic issues. Although there are variations in scheduled caste and non-scheduled caste population, rural-urban scheduled castes and non-scheduled castes but, by and large, about 14 per cent of all respondents belong to younger generation and the other 26 per cent to lower middle age-group (about 40 per cent in total) which was not the case even two decades before. They will accelerate the process of transformation due to their higher level of education, more mobility, and interaction as compared to older generation who resist to change from their age old practices, and adoption of innovations. Therefore, the younger generation specially the educated ones should be encouraged to take the lead in the decision making process of the household matters.

Education is, of course, unfailing engine of change and is the chief instrument through which society socialises its members for bringing desirable change. It is the aggregate of all social process through which people develop abilities, attitudes and other form of behaviour of positive values. Hence, special focus has been given in this study on educational status of the people, and the household, preference of the school and its location for both male and female child. The study reveals that the educational status of the people is not very encouraging because about 49 per cent are illiterate and nearly 43 per cent are less educated. As such nearly 8 per cent are under moderate (7.2%) and highly educated categories (0.7%) taken together. This is mainly due to the fact that majority of the people belong to older or upper-middle generation which neither cared for education due to variety of reasons nor educational infrastructure were available to them during their age of education.

However, there are a lot of variations in the educational status of scheduled castes and non-scheduled castes and the rural-urban components of both the categories. The educational status of scheduled caste shows that about 95 per cent are either illiterate (56%) or less educated (38.5%) with less than 1.5 educational score, leaving only 5 per cent under moderate category (4.86%) and high category (0.36%) together. On the contrary about 85 per cent of non-scheduled castes are either illiterate (29.2%) or less educated (55.78%) leaving only 15 per cent under moderate category (13.1%) and high category (1.76%) put together. It clearly highlights that scheduled castes should not only be given more incentives in various forms and modes but they should be equally encouraged.

There are rural-urban variations in the educational level of both the categories. As expected the rural scheduled castes are less educated than their urban counterpart. But it is not true with non-scheduled castes because about 17 per cent rural non-scheduled castes belong to moderately educated (15.4%) and high educated categories (1.82%), while only 4-5 per cent of urban non-scheduled castes belong to moderate category, and there is none in high category. This is a serious issue which needs to be examined and the urban non-scheduled castes should be given more incentives and encouragement towards education.

The situation is a little more encouraging when the educational status of the households is ascertained by working out the Index of Educational Status wherein the educational score of all the household members have been added together and divided by all household members excluding the children of less than 5 years of age. The result shows that nearly 8 per cent households fall under moderate (7.22%) and high (0.72%) categories of educational index which is nearly 3 per cent more than the total respondents. A closer scrutiny of the master table and questionnaire further indicates that the younger members of the households are not only more educated but are also in the process of acquiring higher education.

The process of social transformation becomes more obvious and encouraging in the analysis of the attitude of the parents regarding the education of their children with respect to two parameters, viz. (i) preference of the location of the school (within the village) and (ii) preference of location of the school (outside the village). The study reveals that the parents are not only willing to educate their children irrespective of the location of school but some of them want to impart quality education in public schools. Nearly 93 per cent of the total masses have expressed the opinion to educate their children (male and female) in government schools within the village/town, while about 7 per cent have shown the desire to educate their children in public schools within the village/town. Interestingly, there has been no distinction in the preferences in case of the male and female child in both the cases. The analysis of data further shows that rural people prefer government schools within the village more than the urban people and *vice versa* is true in case of public schools, which is mainly due to availability of public schools in urban areas as compared to rural areas. Hence, it is suggested that more public schools should be opened in the rural areas. The results regarding the preferences of the government and public schools outside the village is also encouraging in the sense that at least beginning has been made and 205 respondents amounting to about 14 per cent of the total respondents have preferred to send their children outside the village. The large number of people are in favour of government schools because of lesser expenses in it than public schools.

The size of family is an other social parameter, which has undergone a change across the board. Earlier the large size of family was considered as a measure of social security and helpful for generating income but now they have realized the merits and advantages of small and medium size of family which is reflected by the fact that about 22 per cent and 58 per cent (80% both put together) people are covered in these two categories respectively. The other three categories put together account the remaining 20 per cent. However, urban people have an edge over rural people with 78 per cent population under earlier two categories. Hence, it is suggested that rural people still need more education and councilling regarding advantages and merits of small size of family.

The size of family is very much associated with the adoption of family planning programme. The study reveals that the educated younger people are in favour of changing the structure and system of their family. In the ultimate statistical analysis, a little less than one-fifth of the people have gone to the higher category, while more than 30 per cent belong to medium category.

As such 50 per cent people belong to low category. However, as expected, urban people are more receptive to family planning programme than the rural ones.

Marriage is another important social parameter and is very strongly interwoven in the social fabric. But the various related aspects of marriage such as age at marriage, nature of marriage, location of place of marriage, process of marriage, dowry system, etc. have undergone a change. Preference of child marriage, closer distance, within the caste, open dowry demand, ban on widow marriage, etc. are undergoing drastic changes across the board with a little difference among various castes and rural-urban inhabitants. By and large, scheduled castes and rural people have lower level of change as against their counterpart. However, the index of change in the attitude of people towards marriage reveals that about 32 per cent people belong to high category, while nearly 35 per cent fall in the medium category. As such about two-thirds people have higher degree of change leaving only one-third to lower category.

Religion is deeply rooted in Indian social system and has a strong bearing on various other social parameters and economic activities as well. However, in the ultimate statistical analysis it has been found that more than one-fifth people are least religious, while nearly 22 per cent are less religious. As such 58 per cent are either moderately religious or highly religious. However, there are inter-caste and rural-urban variations in level of religiosity. Interestingly, scheduled castes are less religious than non-scheduled castes in case of most of the indicators, but on the whole the urban people are comparatively less religious than rural ones.

Political awareness and involvement is another important indicator of social transformation. The study reveals that the democratic process of elections at various levels has created awakening, interest and involvement among the rural masses. Scheduled castes with their major consolidated vote bank have became conscious about their political rights and privileges. The consolidated processed result indicates that about one-fourth of the population is more aware and involved in political affairs, while about 30 per cent are moderately involved which is a positive sign of social change. Almost similar results have been obtained in case of scheduled castes also but the non-scheduled castes population is a little more involved because of their socio-economic status. The political involvement increases the linkage of the masses with politicians, officers and decision-makers which ultimately helps in their socio-economic well-being. Hence, the masses should be more motivated and encouraged in political affairs but not in politicking.

Closely, related with political involvement is the social mobility, which is a process through which an individual is physically and mentally exposed to the outside of his community. Repeated exposure to new ideas and increasing familiarity with new socio-cultural order accelerates the process of socio-economic transformation. But the picture in this case is not very encouraging. About 66 per cent of the people are less mobile, while 16 per cent are moderately mobile. As such it leaves only 18 per cent in the more mobile category. Lack of means of transportation and lower educational level is, perhaps, the major cause. The study also reveals that the non-scheduled castes population is more mobile than the scheduled castes population with 22 and 16.8 per cent population in moderately and more mobile categories respectively.

However, the composite index of overall social transformation shows that nearly one-fourth of the population belongs to high degree of change with more than 3.5 score, while about one-third come under medium category. As such only 41.5 per cent fall under low category. Hence, the overall hypothesis of social transformation is proved.

Various programmes and policies of rural development in general and agricultural development in particular have resulted into economic prosperity of the masses including the scheduled castes. As a result per capita income across the board has increased. The study reveals that more than one-fourth people belong to high income group, while 38 per cent fall under medium category. As such nearly 60 per cent have reasonable income and the remaining 40 per cent belong to low income group.

Income is the main basis for transformation in other economic parameters such as standard of living, housing condition, exposure to mass media and so on. The index of standard of living indicates that nearly 20 per cent people belong to high category, while

35 per cent fall under medium category. As such 45 per cent have low standard of living and majority of them are scheduled castes in spite of the various government programmes for the upliftment of the rural masses. It is, therefore, suggested that whatever schemes for the upliftment of the rural masses are introduced, they should be properly implemented.

The house is the identity symbol of our social prestige and status. A suitable house influences the physical health, mental efficiency, future skill and productivity which determines the socio-economic status. After independence there has been tremendous improvement in the housing condition across the board in our country. Scheduled castes are spending a lot on the housing. The size, structure, building material, amenities and so on have undergone tremendous change. The index of housing condition based on scoring schemes shows that about 22 per cent people with more than 6 scores live with good housing condition. Nearly half of the masses have moderate housing condition, while 39 per cent have poor houses. This is a very encouraging picture indicating economic change. The housing condition of scheduled castes is poor than non-scheduled castes. The housing condition of 15.5 per cent scheduled castes is good, while in case of non-scheduled castes it is 39 per cent, i.e. almost two and a half time more. Similarly, about 52 per cent scheduled castes have moderate and nearly 32.6 per cent have poor housing condition, while the corresponding percentage in case of non-scheduled castes are 41.7 and 19.1 respectively. It may clearly be inferred that the impact of various rural upliftment and housing programme has not been to the extent it should have been in case of scheduled castes population. Hence, it is suggested that not only more and more housing schemes should be introduced but they should be properly implemented.

Exposure to mass media affects the knowledge, attitude, opinion and behaviour, which in term affects level of adoption of innovations and technology leading to positive economic change. Based on index of change, the study reveals that nearly 45 per cent are more exposed, while nearly 42 per cent are moderately exposed. Only 13 per cent are less exposed which shows that radio, television, news paper, periodicals, etc. have played important role in exposing the masses with the latest developments in various fields not only at national level but also at international levels. The study also reveals that the non-scheduled castes are more exposed than scheduled castes. Therefore, more provisions should be made at various community centres for increasing the level of exposure of the masses.

Occupational structure of the scheduled castes population is one of the major indicators of level of development of a nation. In India, which is basically an agricultural country, agriculture and allied activities are the main occupation of the rural masses. Since the study is basically related with the scheduled castes and few non-scheduled castes, there are few number of cultivators with reasonable size of land holdings. A little more than one-third of the total respondents were actually cultivating the land. Out of these 373 respondents amounting to nearly 59 per cent had marginal size of holding. It clearly indicates the poor status of the people in case of the land holdings. Since the size of holding is small, and people are poor, the level of innovativeness is also low. Kharif and Rabi are the major agricultural seasons with rice, sugarcane, maize, and pulses; and wheat, peas, and vegetables as major crops of each season respectively. The latest trend among the people is the occupational diversification. They are no longer satisfied with one occupation like agriculture, or poultry, or fishing, or labour, or services, etc. but they have adopted more than one occupations. Labour which use to be one of the major economic activities of the people is still important engaging 986 people amounting to 65 per cent of the total but has taken a new form of work contrast in which a group of people take different kind of works anywhere within their commutable distance and complete it within stipulated time period. It is more lucrative to them and tension free for the employer. Dairy farming and fishing engaging 194 and 185 people respectively, are popular occupations being practiced on commercial (189 respondents) and subsistence (190 respondents) basis. It is a main source of income for 34 people, and a subsidiary sources for 155 people. Besides these two, piggeries and poultry farming are other occupations being practiced on commercial and subsistence basis. Hence, apart from agriculture and labour, they are practicing dairy farming, poultry, fishing, piggeries, etc. They are also not only preferring service but are trying hard to get it.

The major change has come in the attitude of the people regarding the preference of the job of their children. They are no longer satisfied with their children being a *daroga, or Lekhpal* but they prefer them to be a doctor, lawyer, civil servant, engineer, teacher, etc. The study reveals that out of 1192 people who have responded to the questions related to the preference of the job of the children, 550 (169 for sons, 381 for daughters) people amounting to nearly 46 per cent have preferred tèaching and 432 (162 for sons, 270 for daughters) covering about 36 per cent have preferred medicine, while 150 and 104 have shown their desire for engineering and civil services respectively. This clearly indicates the higher aspiration and desire of the parents regarding the jobs of their children.

Thus the study reveals the socio-economic transformation of scheduled castes highlighting the differentials among rural and urban, young and old, literate and illiterate, rich and poor and scheduled castes and non-scheduled castes population.

QUESTIONNAIRE

DEPARTMENT OF GEOGRAPHY
DELHI SCHOOL OF ECONOMICS
UNIVERSITY OF DELHI, DELHI-110 007

SOCIO-ECONOMIC TRANSFORMATION OF SCHEDULED CASTES IN UTTAR PRADESH

Schedule No. :________________

Dated :________________

I. Personal and Household Characteristics

1. Name of the Village________________________________
   Block______________ Tehsil___________

2. Name of the respondents __________________ Age ______
   Religion ________________ Caste __________________

3. Education :
   Informal__________________Formal__________________

4. Total Members of Household_________________________

Age Group	< 15		15-30		31-60		60 & Above	
Marital Status	M	F	M	F	M	F	M	F
Members								

II. Farming Characteristics

5. Agricultural Landholdings : Area in __________________

Type of holding	Irrigated	Unirrigated	Total
Land Owned			
Land Leased in : 1. Share 2. Rental			
Land Leased out : 1. Share 2. Rental			

6. Patterns of land use in Kharif Season : Area in__________

Major Crops	Irrigated/Unirrigated	Source of Irrigation	Average Yield

7. Patterns of land use in Rabi Season : Area in__________

Major Crops	Irrigated/Unirrigated	Source of Irrigation	Average Yield

8. Has your cropping pattern changed during last 5 years ? : Yes / No

   If Yes, give details :______________________________

9. Which crops you were growing before ? :________________

10. Has the yield of your crops? : Increased/the same/decreased

11. Adoption of Agricultural Innovations :

A. Farm Implements :

Agricultural Implements	Owned / Hired	Areal Coverage

B. Chemical Fertilizers :

Chemical Fertilizers	Kharif Season			Rabi Season		
	Amount	Crop	Area	Amount	Crop	Area

C. New Varieties of Seed :

Kharif Season		Rabi Season	
Varieties	Area	Varieties	Area

D. Insecticides and Pesticides :

Insecticides and Pesticides	Kharif Season			Rabi Season		
	Amount	Crop	Area	Amount	Crop	Area

III. Educational Level

12. Educational qualification of members who have discontinued education : ______________________

13. Household Educational Level :

Location		Primary I – V		Secondary VI – X	
		Govt. School	Public School	Govt. School	Public School
Within Vill.	M				
	F				
Outside Vill.	M				
	F				

Location		Senior Secondary		Higher Education	
		Govt. School	Public School	Govt. School	Public School
Within Vill.	M				
	F				
Outside Vill.	M				
	F				

14. Where do you prefer your children to study ?

Children	Within Village		Outside Village	
	Govt. School	Public School	Govt. School	Public School
A. Daughter				
B. Son				

15. Why do you prefer Public school ? Better/Nearness/Any Other

16. What would be the order of preference regarding the profession of your children?

Children	Doctor	Engineer	Civil Service	Lawyer	Teacher	Other
Daughter						
Son						

IV. Attitudes Towards Marriage

17. What should be the age at marriage? : Boy__________ Girl________________

18. At what age marriage use to take place :

    a. 5 years before________________
    b. 10 years before________________

19. Where do you want to marry your children: Village/Town/City

20. At what distance the children of your family are married :

    (i) 5 years before: Boys___________ Girls___________

    (ii) 10 years before : Boys_________Girls____________

21. Do you prefer : Arranged/Love/Any other form of marriage

22. Do you like intercaste marriage? Yes/No. Why ? ________________________

23. Do you like the dowry system? Yes / No

24. Does the dowry system prevalent in your family / village ? Yes / No

25. Normally how much do you spent in the marriage of?
    a. Boys : Now_________ 10 Yrs Before________
    b. Girls : Now________ 10 Yrs Before________

26. Do you prefer to marry your children with a person of ?
    (i) Your Profession (ii) Service (iii) Business (iv) Other_

27. Are you aware of family planning programme? Yes/No. If yes, do you practice it ? Yes / No.

28. If you agree at all with it who should adopt it? Husband/Wife

29. Do you favour the adoption of family planning programme? Yes/No

30. Do you think large family is detrimental to economic development? : Yes / No

    Why______________________________

    ____

31. Do you think small family is a happy family?Yes/No. Why____________________

V. **Religiosity**

32. Do you believe in religion? Somewhat/Moderately/Strictly

33. Do you follow the religious rules in your routine life? Somewhat/Moderately/Greatly/Strictly

34. Do you worship regularly as per religious rules? : Yes/No

35. Do you visit religious place outside your village? Never/Rarely/Frequently

36. Do you offer special pooja before taking up new jobs? : Yes/No

37. Do you worship more at the time of hardship and distress? Yes/No

38. Do you believe in religious superstitions? Yes/No

39. Do you attend village religious functions?: Never/Rarely/Frequently

40. Do you go about Janam Patri in deciding about Marriage? Yes/No
Marriage timings : Yes/No Adoption of new jobs : Yes/No
41. Do you consult the priest/religious head on special occasions in the family? :
Never/Rarely/Frequently/Always

42. Do you think that the calamities in our life are result of our KARAM in the past and present life? Yes/No

43. Do you think that all disasters come from God? Yes/No

44. Is there any separate place of worship in your house? : Yes/No

45. Is there any change in your attitudes towards religion? Yes/No

VI. Political Awareness and Involvement

46. What is your assesement of performance of the :
A. Central Government : Good/Satisfactory/Bad/No idea
B. State Government : Good/Satisfactory/Bad/No idea

47. Do you know your?
M.P. :Yes/No Name :______________________
M.L.A.: Yes/No Name :____________________
Chief Minister of the State : Yes/No Name__________
V.L.M. : Yes/No Name______________________

48. Do you go to listen to political leaders when he comes to your area? : Always/Rarely/ Never

49. Do you take active part in organizing political party meetings? Yes/No

50. Have you worked for any party in Assembly Election? Yes/No

If yes, as a Manager/Agent/Convessor/Any Other

51. Do you cast your vote at the time of election?: Regularly/ Rarely/Never

52. Do you think that Kargil war is our own creation? : Yes/No

53. Do you consider Ms. Mayawati as National or Regional Leader? ______________

54. Whom would you prefer as C.M. of U.P.? Mayawati/ Kanshi Ram/Kalyan Singh/Mulayam Singh

55. Do you like frequent holding of elections? : Yes/No

56. Do you think that the collusion government will be successful? Yes/No

57. Have you visited the following while in session?
    A. State Assembly : Never/Rarely/Frequently
    B. Rajya Sabha : Never/Rarely/Frequently
    C. Parliament : Never/Rarely/Frequently

58. Are you aware of P.M's Lahore Bus Journey? Yes/No

VII. Social Mobility

59. Normally how many times do you visit your friend/relatives outside village in a year if it is at a distance of :
    Less than 5 Kms.____________ 5-10 Kms.____________
    More than 10 Kms. ________

60. Normally how many times do you visit your relations in a year? :
    Less than 5 Kms.______ 5-10 Kms.________
    More than 10 Kms.. __________

61. Normally how many times do you contact the following in a year? :
    M.P.______M.L.A.______B.D.O.________
    V.L.W._______Lekhpal________

62. How do you go to these people?: Now a days______;10 yrs before___________

63. Has your mode of transport changed during the last decade? Yes/No
If yes, what was it before? ___________________________

64. Do you visit the periodic market? Regularly/Rarely/Never

65. Do you visit Fair and Exhibitions? Regularly/Rarely/Never

VIII. Housing Condition

66. No. of houses : A. Living House___________________
B. Cattle Shed_____________

67. Type of houses : Kuchha_______Pucca________Kuchha-Pucca_______

68. Approximate Area of house : Living House_________
Compound: ____________

69. Building Materials: ________________________________

70. Have you built it yourself or inherited it? :______________

71. It is single storied/double stories: _________________

72. The year and approximate cost of construction: Year________Cost__________

73. How many rooms are there?: _________________________

74. Is there a separate :(i) Kitchen (Yes/No) (ii) Bathroom (Yes/No) (iii) Guest room (Yes/No) (iv) Toilet (Yes/No) (v) Cattle shed (Yes/No)

75. Do you have : Chairs (Yes/No); Sofa Set (Yes/No); Table (Yes/No)

76. Have you taken electricity connection? Yes/No
If yes, Do you have : Fan (Yes/No); Tubelight (Yes/No); Electric Press (Yes/No); Freeze (Yes/No); Heater (Yes/No); Any Other__________

77. Do you have sewing machine? Yes/No, If yes : Year of purchase__________

78. Which utensils do you use?: Aluminium/Steel/Hindalium/China clay; All of these.

79. Which cooking fuel do you use?: Wood/Cowdung/Coal/ Oil

80. What is the source of your drinking water?: Tube Well/ Well/ Handpump/Tank

81. Interviewer's assessment of it: ________________________

IX. Exposure to Mass Media

82. Do you have Radio/Transistor?: Yes/No. If yes, year of purchase____________

83. If no, do you listen to elsewhere? Frequently/Rarely/Never

84. Do you listen to Krishi Darshan Programme?: Yes/No/ Never/Rarely/Frequently

85. Do you have a T.V. set? Yes/No. If yes, year of purchase__________________

86. If no, do you watch from your neighbour? Never/Rarely/Frequently

87. Do you watch Rural Development Programme?: Never/ Rarely/Frequently

88. Do you go to movie? Yes/No. If yes, place and frequency________________

89. Do you subscribe/Buy Newspaper?: Yes/No. If yes, Name________________

90. If no, do you read it from elsewhere? : Never/Rarely/ Frequently

91. Does it provide information about upliftment of S.C.?: None/ Little/A lot

X. Means of Transport

92. Do you have: (i) Bicycle (Yes/No); (ii) Motorcycle (Yes/No); (iii) Car (Yes/No); Bullock cart (Yes/No); (iv) Any other means____________

93. When did you purchase it?: ________________________

94. What is your most common means of transport?: ________________________

XI. Occupational Transformation

95. Do you practice dairy farming? Yes/No. If yes, since when?_______________

96a. Animals detail :

Animal Details	Number	Age	Amount of Milk	Milching Period	Remarks
Cow					
Buffaloes					

b. Commercial/Subsistence Basic : ____________________

c. Main Source/Subsidiary Source : ____________________

d. Average income per month: ____________________

e. Place of sale of milk and milk product: ________________

f. Do you also purchase and sale milk?: Yes/No. If yes, details_____________

g. Place of purchase______ Place of sale______Income______

h. Have you started keeping new breeds? Yes/No. If yes, Name the breed_____

i. Is it more profitabile?: Yes/No. _______________________

j. What are problems in it?: ____________________________

97a.Do you practice Piggeries? Yes/No. If yes, since when____________________

b. Commercial/Subsistence/Main source/Subsidiary Source ______________

c. Average income per month from it: ____________

d. Where and how do you sell its products: __________

e. Do you have rare new Breeds? Yes/No. Name_______ Profitability Level: ___________

f. Major problems in it: ______________________

98a. Do you practice fishing? Yes/No. If yes, since when______________________

b. Commercial/Subsistence Basis: __________________

c. Main/Subsidiary Source: ______________________

d. Where do you sell it?: ________________________

e. Peak season of fishing : Summer/Winter/Rainy Season

f. Do you purchase and sell fishes?: Give details_____________________________

g. What are the major problems in it?: ______________________

h. Do you take the contract of the village water bodies?: Yes / No

i. If yes, how much do you earn from it?: ______________________

99a. Do you practice poultry farming ? Yes/No. If yes, since when______________
b. Commercial/Subsistence Basis: ______________
c. Main Source/Subsidiary Source: ______________
d. Average income per month from it: ______________
e. Where do you sell its products?: ______________
f. Do you also purchase and sell poultry products?: Yes/No
g. What are the new breeds you have?: ______________
h. What are the major problems in it?: ______________

XII. Other Occupations

100.a. Is there any member of your family in service?: Yes / No
If yes,

Member	Nature of Job	Place of Work	Distance	Monthly Salary

b. Does he stay at place of work? Yes/No. If yes
i. Alone, How much money remits?: ______________
ii. With family : How much money remits in a month?:______

c. Is there any member working outside village other than service. If yes,

Memebr	Nature of Job	Place of Work	Distance	Monthly Salary

d. Does he live with family or alone? Family/Alone
e. How much money does he remits to you monthly?____________________________

101. Does labour is your main occupation? : Yes/No

a. Where do you practice it? : Within village/Outside village/Both Places
b. Do you go as seasonal labourer outside of your village? : Yes/No
c. If yes, how much do you earn in a season?: ____________________________
d. Do you work as: Agricultural Labourers/Construction Labourers/Any other labour
e. Do you practice labour on : Daily wages basis/Contract basis
f. If daily wages basis, how much you get in a day?: ________________________
g. If contract basis, do you work individually/As a team: ________________________
h. Is it more profitable?: ____________________________

102. Do you think that during last two decades your :

a. Annual income : Increased/the same/decreased
b. Economic Condition : Improved/the same/decreased
c. Social Status : Improved/the same/decreased
d. Mobility : Improved/the same/decreased
e. Religiosity : Improved/the same/ decreased
f. Family educational level : Increased/the same/ decreased
g. Housing Condition : Improved/the same/ decreased
h. Level of exposure : Increased/the same/ decreased
i. Agricultural Production : Increased/the same/ decreased
j. Agricultural Technology : Increased/the same/ decreased

XIII. Remarks by the Surveyor

____

____

____

____

____

____

____

____

BIBLIOGRAPHY

Alexander, K.C., 1958 : *Social Mobility in Kerala,* Uppal Publishing House, Delhi.

Alexender, J.C., 1990 : *Culture and Society : Contemporary Debate,* Cambridge University Press, Cambridge.

Ambedkar, B.R., 1946 : *Who Were the Sudras?* Thackers Publications, Bombay.

Ambedkar, B.R., 1948 : *The Untouchables*, Amrit Book Co., New Delhi.

Asia Development Bank, 2001 : *Growth and Change in Asia and the Pacific, (Key Indicators),* Oxford University Press, London.

Auden, J.B. and Roy, P.C., 1942 : 'Report on the Sodium Salt in Reh in the U.P.', *Records of the Geological Survey of India,* Professional Paper No. 1, Calcutta.

Baily, K.D., 1994 : *Methods of Social Research,* Free Press, New York.

Bhardwaj, A.N., 1979 : *The Problems of Scheduled Castes and Scheduled Tribes in India,* Light and Life Pub., New Delhi.

Bhat, A., 1975 : *Caste, Class and Politics,* Delhi.

Bhatia, B.M., 1977 : *Poverty, Agriculture and Economic Growth,* Vikas, New Delhi.

Bhatnagar, A., 1990 : *A Scheduled Caste in an Urban Setting – The Jatav Chamars of Dehra Dun City.*

Blaikic, M., 2000 : *Designing Social Research,* Polity Press, Cambrdige.

Blandford, H.F., 1889 : *Climate and Weather of India, Ceylon and Burma*, London.

Blanford, H.F., 1886-88 : 'The Rainfal of India', *Memmoirs of India Meteorological Department,* Vol. III, New Delhi.

Bose, S.P., 1961 : Characteristics of Farmers Who Adopt Agricultural Practices in Indian Villages, *Rural Sociology,* Vol. 26.

Brishni, R.W., 1973 : *Cross Cultural Research Methods,* John Wiley, New York.

Brown, Lester R., 1971 : *Social Impact of the Green Revolution,* Coarnegie, New York.

Bumble, M.D., 1983 : *Deprived Castes and their Struggle for Equality,* Ashish Publishing House, Delhi.

Burrard, S.G., 1912 : 'On the Origin of Himalayan Mountain', *Geological Survey of India,* Professional Paper No. 12, Calcutta.

Chakravarti, A., 2001 : *Social Power and Everyday Class Relations : Agrarian Transformation in North Bihar.*

Chopra, K. and Gulati, S.C., 2001 : *Migration, Common Property Resources and Environmental Degradation : Interlinkages in India's Arid and Semi-arid Regions,* Institute of Economic Growth, Delhi.

Crook, W., 1974 : *The Tribes and Castes of North Western Provinces,* Vol. I-IV.

Danda, A.K., 1993 : *Weaker Sections in Indian Villages,* Inter India Pub., New Delhi.

Desai, D.K., 1966 : Technological Change and its Diffusion in Agriculture, *Indian Journal of Agricultural Economics,* No. 1, Vol. XXI.

Doi, K., 1957: The Industrial Structure of Japanese Prefecture, *Proceedings of I.G.U. Regional Conference,* Japan.

Dreze, J. and Kingdon, G., 2001 : 'School Participation in Rural India', *Review of Development Economics,* 5.

Duty, N.K., 1931 : *Origin and Growth of Caste in India,* Calcutta.

Everett, J.M., 1981 : *Women and Social Change in India,* Heritage Pub., Delhi.

Farro, T.J., 2001 : *Social Action System and Synthesis in Sociological Theory,* Preger, Westport.

Ghurye, G.S., 1961 : *Caste, Class and Occupation,* Popular Book Depot, Bombay.

Gore, M. S., 1985 : *Social Aspect of Development,* Rawat Pub., Jaipur.

Gregory, R.J., 2003 : Tribes and Tribal : Origin, Use and Future of the Concept, *Studies of Tribes and Trebles,* Vol. 1, Delhi.

Grigg, D.B., 1984 : *An Introduction to Agricultural Geography,* London.

Hanumantha Rao, C.H. and Linneman, (eds.), 1996 : Economic Reforms and Poverty Alleviation in India : *Indo-Dutch Studies on Development Alternatives,* Vol. 17.

Harrison, A.J., 1977 : *Economics and Landuse Planning,* London.

Harvey, D.W., 1966 : Theoretical Concepts and the Analysis of Agricultural Landuse Patterns in Geography. *Ann. Ass. Am. Geographers,* p. 56.

Harvey, D.W., 1969 : *Explanations in Geography,* Arnold, London.

Hayami, R. and Ruttan, V., 1971 : *Agricultural Development : An International Perspective,* Johns Hopkins Press, Baltimore, pp. 67-85.

Hoda, A., 2002 : 'WTO Agreement on Agriculture and India', in Hoda, A. (ed.), *WTO Agreement and Indian Agriculture,* Social Science Press, Delhi.

Joshi, B.R. 1982 : *Democracy in Search of Equality : Untouchable Politics and Indian Social Change,* Hindustan Pub. Co., Delhi.

Joshi, B.R., 1986 : *Untouchable — Voice of Dalit Liberation Movement,* Select Book Service, Syndicate.

Joshi, P.C., 1989 : *Culture, Communication and Social Change,* Vikas Pub., New Delhi.

Kabilan, R., 1993 : *From Traditional Society to Post Industrial Society,* Common Wealth Pub., New Delhi.

Kahkonen, S. and Olson, M. (eds.) 2001 : *A New Institutional Approach to Economic Development.*

Kendrew, W.G., 1961 : *The Climates of the Continents,* Oxford.

Khusro, A.M., 1973 : *The Economics of Land Reforms and Farm Size in India,* McMillan, Madras.

Kingdon, G., 1996 : 'The Quality and Efficiency of Private and Public Education : A Case Study of Urban India', *Oxford Bulletin of Economics and Statistics,* 58(1), 57-82.

Kothari, C.R., 1990 : *Research Methodology, Methods and Techniques,* Second ed. Wiley Eastern, New Delhi.

Krishanji, N. and Krishnan, T.N. (eds.) 2000 : Public Support for Food Security : The Public Distribution System in India. *Strategies for Human Development in India,* Vol. 1.

Krishnan, M.S., 1960 : *Geology of India and Burma,* Madras.

Shirsagar, R.K., 1994 : *Dalit Movement in India and its Leaders,* M.D. Publishers, Delhi.

Kulkarni, K.M., 1977 : Micro Level Variations in Economic Development in Rajasthan, *Indian Journal of Regional Science,* No. 2, Vol. 9.

Kumar, P., 1991 : *Poverty, Election and Rural Hrijans,* Discovery Publishing House, New Delhi.

Kundu, A., 1975 : Construction of Composite Indices for Regional Analysis —An Enquiry in the Methods of Analysis, *Geographical Review of India* (1) Vol. 37, Calcutta.

Kuznets, S., 1973 : 'Modern Economic Growth : Findings and Reflections', *American Economic Review,* 13(3), 247-258.

Lal, A.K. and Tiwari, S.N., 1977 : *The Harijan Elite,* Thompson Pub., Faridabad.

Lees, E.S., 1966 : A Theory of Migration, *Demography,* Vol. 3.

Lynch, O.M., 1969 : *The Politics of Untouchables,* National Pub., Delhi.

Majeed, A., 1992 : 'Crop-Combinational Analysis : A Review in Methodology, in Mohammad, N.(ed.), *New Dimensions in Agricultural Geography,* Vol. V., Concept Pub. Co., New Delhi.

Massey, J., 1995 : *Dalits in India,* Manohar Pub., Delhi.

Mathew, J., 1986 : *Ideology, Protest and Social Mobility : Case Studies of Mhars and Pulayas,* Inter India Pub., New Delhi.

McGranahan, D., Pizarro, E. and Richard, C., 1985 : *Measurement and Analysis of Socio-economic Development,* N.N. Research Institute, Geneva.

Mehrotra, C.L., 1972 : "Soils of Uttar Pradesh, Their Broad Distribution and Management", *Fertilizer News.*

Mohammad, N., 1989 : *Impact of Caste on Primary Occupations : A Geographical Analysis,* Concept Publishing Co., New Delhi.

Mohammad, N., 2000 : Socio-economic Transformation of Scheduled Caste in Eastern Uttar Pradesh : A Geographical Analysis, in Singh, D.K., Dube, R.S. and Srivastava, V.K. (eds.) *Geography, Development and Change,* Association of Marketing Geographers of India, Gorakhpur.

Mohammad, N., and Pathania, A., 1997 : 'Spatial Inequality in Man-Land Ratio in India' in Akhtar, R. (ed.) *Contemporary Approaches to Indian Geography,* APH Pub., Delhi.

Mohammad, N., 1978 : *Agricultural Land use in India,* Inter-India Publication, Delhi.

Mohammad, N., 1978 : Impact of Economic Factors on Diffusion of Agricultural Innovations in Central Trans-Ghaghara Plain, *Geographical Review of India,* Vol. XL, Calcutta.

Mohammad, N., 1978 : 'Impact of Social Factors on Diffusion of Agricultural Innovation in Central Trans-Ghaghara Plain', *National Geographical Journal of India,* Vol. XXIV, Varanasi.

Mohammad, N., and Majeed, A., 1979 : 'Socio-Economic Factors and Diffusions of Agricultural Innovation' in Ali Mohammad (ed.), *Dynamics of Agricultural Development in India,* Concept Pub. Co., New Delhi.

Mohammad, N., 1992 : 'Pattern of Agricultural Landuse in Ghaghara-Rapti Doab' in Mohammad, N. (ed.), *New Dimensions in Agricultural Geography,* Vol. V., Concept Pub. Co., New Delhi.

Mohammad, N., 1992 : 'Spatial Variations in Levels of Development in U.P. in Mohammad, N., (ed.) *Dynamics of Agricultural Development,* Concept Pub. Co., New Delhi.

Mukherjee, A.B., 1980 : *The Chamars of Uttar Pradesh,* Concept Publishing Co., New Delhi.

Nartu, P., 2001 : *Dynamics of Social Structure and Change,* Dnam. Co. Pub., Delhi.

Newman, W.L., 1997 : *Social Research Methods : Qualitative and Quantitative Approach,* Allen and Becon, Boston.

Oldham, R.D. 1917 : 'The Structure of Himalayas and Gangetic Plain', *Memoirs of the Geological Survey of India,* Vol. XLII, Pt. II, Calcutta.

Pal, M.N., 1975 : Regional Disparities in the Levels of Development, *Indian Journal of Regional Science,* Vol. II, No. 1.

Pal., M.N., 1962 : *Composite Index of Economic Development : A Method of Regional Analysis of Economic Development with Special Reference to South India,* Regional Survey Unit, Indian Statistical Institute, New Delhi.

Panse, V.G. and Singh, D., 1966 : Promotion and Assessment of Technological Change in Indian Agriculture, *Indian Journal of Agricultural Economics,* Vol. XXI.

Parvathamma, C., 1989 : *Scheduled Castes at the Cross Road,* Ashish Publishing House, Delhi.

Parvathamma, C., and Satyanarayana, 1984 : *New Horizons and Scheduled Castes,* Ashish Publishing House, Delhi.

Pasachropoulos, G., 1988 : 'Education and Development : A Review', *World Bank Research Observer,* 3(1), 99-116.

Pathak, Bindeshwar, *Continuity and Change in Indian Society,* Concept Publishing Co., New Delhi.

Patwardhan, S., 1973 : *Changes Among India's Harijans,* Orient Longman, New Delhi.

Prabhu Seeta, K., 2001 : *Economic Reform and Social Sector Development : A Study of Two Indian States,* UNDP India Country Office, New Delhi.

Pradhan, A.C., 1989 : *The Emergence of the Depressed Classes,* Bookland International, Bhubaneshwar.

Prakash, B.A. (ed.), 1999 : *Kerala's Economic Development; Issues and Problems,* University of Kerala, Thiruvananthapuram.

Prakash, N., 1989 : *Scheduled Castes : Socio-Economic Change,* Chugh Pub., Allahabad.

Rahudkwar, W.P., 1962 : Farmer's Characteristic Associated with the Adoption and Diffusion of Improved Farm Practices, *Indian Journal of Agricultural Economics,* Vol. XVII.

Rangaswamy, P., *et al.*, 1972 : *India's Changing Farmers,* Allahabad.

Rani, U., 1971 : 'Farm Size and Productivity', *Economic and Political Weekly,* June, pp. A85-A89.

Raychaudhari, S.P. *et al.,* 1962 : *Soils of India,* New Delhi.

Raychaudhari, S.P. and Mukerjee, S.K., 1947 : *Present Position of Soil Survey in India*, J.S.I.R.

Raza, M., 1992 : *Development and Ecology*, Rawat Publications, Jaipur.

Reynolds, L., 1983 : 'Innovations and Adjustments in Economic Growth', *Swedish Journal of Economics,* 74(4), 431-451.

Rogaly, B. and Barbara Harriss-White, Bose, S. (eds.), 1999 : *Sonar Bangla?* Agricultural Growth and Agrarian Change in West Bengal and Bangladesh.

Roy Burman, B.K., 1994 (a) : *Tribes in Perspective,* Mittal Publications, Delhi.

Roy, R. and Singh, V.B., 1987 : *Between Two World : A Study of Harijan Elites,* Discovery Pub. House, Delhi.

Salve, R.S., 1966 : 'Technological Change in Agricultural Development : Role of Irrigation on Cropping Pattern', *Indian Journal of Agricultural Economics,* Vol. XXI.

Sathyamurthy, T.V., *Class Transformation and Practical Transformation in Post Colonial India,* New Delhi.

Selvanathan, S., 1989 : *Status of Scheduled Castes,* Ashish Publishing House, Delhi.

Shafi, M., 1960 : *Land Utilization in Eastern Uttar Pradesh,* Alligarh.

Shafi, M., 1984 : *Agricultural Productivity and Regional Imbalances,* Concept Publishing Company, New Delhi.

Sharma, A.C., *1976 : Mechanisation of Punjab Agriculture,* New Delhi.

Sharma, K.L., 1968 : 'Level of Mobility in Caste Structure –A Hypothetical Refinement', *The Indian Journal of Social Work,* Vol. XXXII, No. 4.

Sharma, N., 1985 : *Untouchables in Rural Gujarat,* Popular Prakashan, Bombay.

Sharma, R.S. 1958 : *Sudras in Ancient India,* Delhi.

Sharma, S., 1986 : *The Chamar Artisans,* B.R. Pub., New Delhi.

Shetty, M.S., 1966 : Inter-Farm Rate of Technological Diffusion in Indian Agriculture, *Indian Journal of Agricultural Economics,* Vol. XXI.

Shiva, V. and Bedi, G. (eds.), 2002 : *Sustainable Agriculture and Food Security : The Impact of Globalisation.*

Shiva, V., 1991 : *The Violence of Green Cultivation,* Mapusa, Goa.

Shukla, K.S. and Verma, B.M., 1993 : *Development of Scheduled Castes and Administration,* Uppal Publishing House, Delhi.

Singh, J., 1974 : *The Green Revolution in India – How Green it is?* (Kurukshetra).

Singh, D.R., 1985 : *Rural Leadership Among Scheduled Castes,* Chugh Pub., Allahabad.

Singh, J., 1984 : *Agricultural Geography,* Tata McGraw Hill Pub. Co., New Delhi.

Singh, J. and Dhillon, S.S., 1994 : *Agricultural Geography,* Tata McGraw Hill Pub. Co., New Delhi.

Singh, R.P., 1992 : 'Concept of Landuse' in Mohammad, N. (ed.) *New Dimensions in Agricultural Geography,* Vol. IV, Concept Pub. Co., New Delhi.

Sinha, A., 1982 : *Caste System: Myths, Reality, Challenge,* New Delhi.

Sinha, S., 1977 : *The Harijan Elite,* Thompson Press Ltd., Delhi.

Sinha, Sachchidanand, 1988 : *Social Change in Village India,* Concept Publishing Co., New Delhi.

Spate, O.H.K. and Learmonth, A.T.A., 1967 : *India and Pakistan,* London.

Stern, R.W., 1993 : *Changing India,* Cambridge Univesrity Press, New Delhi.

Strauss, A. and Gornin, J., 1999 : *Basics of Qualitative Research – Grounden Theory Practice and Techniques,* Sage Pub., New Delhi.

Subbiah, S. and Ahmad, A., 1980 : Determinants of Agricultural Productivity in Tamil Nadu — India, *Transaction of Institute of Indian Geographers,* No. 1, Vol. II, pp. 19-32.

Sundaram, K., and Tendulkar, S.D., 1988 : *Measurement of Poverty : Some Conceptual Problems*, Paper No. 36, Second Seminar on Social Statistics, Feb. 4-6, 1988, Central Statistical Organisation, New Delhi.

Tendulkar, S.D., 1992 : 'Economic Growth and Poverty', in Hariss, B., Guhan, S. and Cassen, R.(eds.) *Poverty in India : Research and Policy,* Oxford University Press, Bombay, I, Sections III and IV, pp. 32-42.

The World Bank, 1990 : *World Development Indicator,* Washington D.C.

Tornquist, O., 1999 : *Politics and Development : A Critical Introduction,* Uppsala University.

Trewarth, G.T., 1962 : *The Earth's Problem Climate,* London.

Tripathi, R.B., 1994 : *Dalit : A Sub Human Society,* Ashish Publishing House, Delhi.

Vajpaeyi, K., 1979 : *Modernisation and Social Change in India,* Manohar Pub., New Delhi.

Vidyarthi, L.P. and Mishra, M., 1979 : *Harijan Today : Socio-economic, Political, Religious and Cultural Analysis,* Classical Publishing, New Delhi.

Wadia, D.N. and Auden, J.B., 1939 : Geology and Structure of Northern India, *Memoirs of the Geological Survey of India,* Vol. LXXIII, Delhi.

Wadia, D.N., 1976 : *Geology of India,* Delhi.

Weaver, J.C., 1954 : Crop-Combination Regions in Middle-West, *The Geographical Review,* Vol. XLIV.

Wilkening, E.H., 1950 : A Socio-Psychological Approach to the Study of Acceptance of Innovations in Farming, *Rural Sociology.*

World Bank, 1997 : *World Development Report, 1997,* Washington D.C., World Bank.

Yadav, S.K., 1983 : *Harijan Awareness of Educational Scheme,* Academy Press, Gurgaon.

Zellion, E., 1992 : *From Untouchables to Dalit : Essays in Ambedkar Movement,* Manohar Pub., New Delhi.

Zhianska, L. and Dinitrova, M., 1986 : *Society and Social Change,* Svyat Pub., Safia.

INDEX